M000074730

OPERA JOURNEYS LIBRETTO SERIES

Rossini's

THE BARBER OF SEVILLE

TRANSLATED FROM ITALIAN
and including music highlight transcriptions

Edited by Burton D. Fisher
Principal lecturer, *Opera Journeys Lecture Series*

Opera Journeys Publishing™ / Miami, Florida

WEB SITE: www.operajourneys.com   E MAIL: operaj@bellsouth.net

THE BARBER OF SEVILLE

"Il Barbiere di Siviglia"

Opera in Italian in two acts

Music by Gioacchino Rossini

Libretto by Cesare Sterbini,

adapted from the play by Beaumarchais,

***Le Barbier de Séville* (1775)**

Premiere in Rome, February 1816.

Principal Characters in THE BARBER OF SEVILLE

Count Almaviva, a nobleman	Tenor
Figaro, a factotum	Baritone
Rosina, the ward of Dr. Bartolo	Soprano
Dr. Bartolo, Rosina's guardian	Bass
Don Basilio, a music teacher	Bass
Fiorello, a servant of the Count	Bass
Berta, a servant of Dr. Bartolo	Mezzo-soprano
Ambrosio, a servant of Dr. Bartolo	Tenor

Officer, soldiers, policemen, a notary

TIME: 17th century

PLACE: Seville, Spain

Brief Story Synopsis

The young and beautiful Rosina is the ward of the elderly Dr. Bartolo, her jealous guardian who shelters her in virtual imprisonment and insulates her from the outside world, and plans to marry her so he can secure her dowry. The young Count Almaviva has seen Rosina and become bewitched by her charms. Rosina likewise becomes enamored by the Count, a man she believes is a poor student named Lindoro.

Obsessed to meet Rosina, the Count hires Figaro, Seville's famous factotum, barber, and jack-of-all trades, who plans an intrigue that will enable him to enter Dr. Bartolo's house.

First the Count is disguised as a soldier who demands to be billeted in Bartolo's house. He manages to make himself known to Rosina, exchanges letters with her, but escapes arrest by making his true identity known to soldiers.

Afterwards the Count disguises himself as Don Alonso, a music teacher substituting for the supposedly ill Don Basilio. When Don Basilio suddenly appears, Figaro persuades him that he has a raging fever, and inspired by a purse he surreptitiously receives from the Count, he dismisses himself. But Bartolo discovers the charade and the intrigue fails.

Figaro has obtained the balcony key, and together with the Count, arrives at midnight to rescue Rosina. After they arrive, their plan is thwarted when they discover that their ladder has disappeared. But when Basilio arrives with the notary, he is persuaded by the point of a gun to witness the marriage between Rosina and the Count.

Although seething at his loss, Dr. Bartolo is content when the Count gives him Rosina's dowry. In this war between rivals for the hand of Rosina, all of Bartolo's efforts were in vain: useless precautions. In the end, Bartolo showers the young lovers with his blessings for their happiness.

ACT I

*An open square in Seville at dawn. Dr. Bartolo's house is visible,
its windows barred, and its shutters closed.
With a lantern in his hands, Fiorello, a servant of Count Almaviva,
ushers a group of musicians in front of the house, followed by the Count.*

FIORELLO:
Piano, pianissimo, senza parlar,
tutti con me venite qua.

FIORELLO: *(advancing cautiously)*
Quiet, very quiet, and don't talk,
all of you come here with me.

SUONATORI:
Piano, pianissimo, eccoci qua.

MUSICIANS:
We're here, be quiet, be very quiet.

TUTTI:
Tutto è silenzio; nessun qui sta
che i nostri canti possa turbar.

ALL:
It's so quiet; there's no one here who can
disturb our songs.

CONTE:
Fiorello, olà!

COUNT: *(whispering to Fiorello)*
Fiorello, hello!

FIORELLO:
Signor son qua.

FIORELLO:
I'm here, my lord.

CONTE:
Ebben! Gli amici?

COUNT:
Where are our friends?

FIORELLO:
Son pronti gà.

FIORELLO:
They're already here.

CONTE:
Bravi, bravissimi, fate silenzio;
piano, pianissimo, senza parlar.

COUNT:
Wonderful, terrific. Tell them to be quiet,
very quiet, and no talking.

SUONATORI:
Piano, pianissimo, senza parlar.

MUSICIANS:
Quiet, very quiet, and no talking.

The musicians tune their instruments, and then accompany the Count in a serenade.

Largo
COUNT ALMAVIVA

Ec - co ri - den - te in cie - lo

CONTE:
Ecco, ridente in cielo
spunta la bella aurora,
e tu non sorgi ancora
e puoi dormir così?
Sorgi, mia dolce speme,
vieni, bell'idol mio;
rendi men crudo, oh Dio!

Io stral che mi ferì.
Oh sorte! Già veggo
quel caro sembiante;
quest'anima amante
ottenne pietà.

Oh istante d'amore!
Oh dolce contento!
Soave momento
che eguale non ha!

Ehi, Fiorello?

FIORELLO:
Mio Signore!

CONTE:
Dì, la vedi?

FIORELLO:
Signor no.

CONTE:
Ah, ch'è vana ogni speranza!

FIORELLO:
Signor Conte, il giorno avanza.

CONTE:
Ah! Che penso! Che farò?
Tutto è vano buona gente!

SUONATORI:
Mio signor

CONTE:
Avanti, avanti.

COUNT:
Here, the sky smiles as it
brings the early dawn.
Why are you still sleeping?
Why don't you get up?
Wake up, my hope,
come, my beautiful treasure;
oh God, don't be so cruel!

I am wounded by a darting arrow.
Such a fate! I can't wait
to see that beautiful vision;
this loving soul
deserved to be pitied.

Blissful moment of love!
Sweet contentment!
Nothing can rival
this gentle moment!

Hey, Fiorello?

FIORELLO:
My lord!

COUNT:
Have you seen her?

FIORELLO:
No my lord.

COUNT:
My hopes are in vain!

FIORELLO:
My lord, dawn is arriving.

COUNT:
How sad! What shall I do?
Good friends, all is in vain!

MUSICIANS:
My lord.

COUNT:
Come closer.

The Count gives a purse to Fiorello, who distributes the money among the musicians.

Più di suoni, più di canti io bisogno omai
non ho.

Here is my appreciation but I no longer
need your music.

FIORELLO:
Buona notte a tutti quanti,
più di voi che far non so.

FIORELLO:
Good night to all of you,
we no longer need your services.

The musicians surround the Count, thank him profusely, kissing his hand and his cloak.
Annoyed by their noisy demonstration, the Count and Fiorello chase them away.

SUONATORI:
Mille grazie mio signore
del favore dell'onore.
Ah, di tanta cortesia obbligati in verità.
Oh, che incontro fortunato!
È un signor di qualità.

MUSICIANS:
My lord, a thousand thanks for the honor
and your generosity.
We are so grateful for your courtesy.
How fortunate we are to know you!
You are a man of honor!

CONTE:
Basta, basta, non parlate,
Ma non serve, non gridate.
Maledetti, andate via.
Ah, canaglia, via di qua.
Tutto quanto il vicinato
questo chiasso sveglierà.

COUNT:
Enough, enough, stop talking,
stop patronizing, stop shouting.
Damned you, go away.
Go away you rabble.
This noise will awaken
the entire neighborhood.

FIORELLO:
Zitti, zitti che rumore!
Maledetti, via di qua!
Ve' che chiasso indiavolato!
Ah, che rabbia che mi fa!

FIORELLO:
Silence, silence that uproar!
Damned you, get away from here!
What a devilish uproar!
You're making me angry!

The musicians finally leave.

CONTE:
Gente indiscreta!

COUNT:
What indiscreet people!

FIORELLO:
Ah, quasi con quel chiasso importuno
tutto quanto il quartiere han risvegliato.
Alfin sono partiti!

FIORELLO:
Their annoying noise has almost
awakened the whole neighborhood.
But they've finally gone!

CONTE:
E non si vede!
È inutile sperar.

COUNT: *(looking toward the balcony)*
I don't see her!
It's useless to wait!

The Count paces back and forth, reflecting on his dilemma.

(Eppur qui voglio aspettar di vederla. Ogni mattina ella su quel balcone a prender fresco viene sull'aurora.Proviamo.)

(Yet I must wait to see her. Every morning she comes out on the balcony to breathe the fresh dawn air. We'll have to try again.)

Olà, tu ancora ritirati, Fiorel.

Listen Fiorello, you can leave now.

FIORELLO:
Vado.
Là in fondo attenderò suoi ordini.

FIORELLO:
I'm going.
I'll be over there awaiting your orders.

Fiorello departs.

CONTE:
Con lei se parlar mi riesce,
non voglio testimoni.
Che a quest'ora io tutti i giorni qui vengo
per lei dev'essersi avveduta.
Oh, vedi, amore a un uomo del mio rango
come l'ha fatta bella!
Eppure, eppure! Dev'essere mia sposa.

COUNT:
If I can see her just one moment, I don't
need a witness.
She has seen me every morning waiting
under her window.
Look at what love has done to a man of my
stature!
Hurry, you must become my wife.

In the distance, Figaro is heard approaching, singing merrily.

Chi è mai quest'importuno?
Lasciamolo passar; sotto quegli archi,
non veduto, vedrò quanto bisogna;
già l'alba appare e amor non si vergogna.

Who can this intruder be?
I'll hide under that arch and let him pass.
I won't be seen but I'll see what I must.
It is already dawn and my love has still has
not appeared.

As the Count hides, Figaro appears, his guitar hanging from his neck.

Allegro vivace
FIGARO

Lar - go al fac - to - tum del-la cit - tà, lar - go!

FIGARO:
Largo al factotum della città!
Presto a bottega, che' l'alba è già.

Ah, che bel vivere, che bel piacere
per un barbiere di qualità!

FIGARO:
Make way for the city's great factotum!
It's already morning, and I'm ready for
business.
What a great life, what pleasures an
excellent barber has!

Ah, bravo Figaro!
Bravo, bravissimo; fortunatissimo
per verità!
Pronto a far tutto, la notte e il giorno
sempre d'intorno, in giro sta.

Miglior cuccagna per un barbiere, vita più
nobile, no, non si dà.
Rasori e pettini, lancette e forbici,
al mio comando tutto qui sta.

V'è la risorsa, poi, del mestiere
colla donnetta col cavaliere.
Ah, che bel vivere, che bel piacere
per un barbiere di qualità!

Tutti mi chiedono, tutti mi vogliono,
donne, ragazzi, vecchi, fanciulle:
Qua la parrucca, presto la barba,
qua la sanguigna, presto il biglietto.

Figaro, Figaro!.
Son qua, son qua.
Figaro, Figaro!
Eccomi qua.
Ahimè! Che furia!
Ahimè! Che folla!

Uno alla volta, per carità!
Pronto prontissimo son come il fulmine:
sono il factotum della città.
Ah, bravo Figaro!
Bravo, bravissimo;
a te fortuna non mancherò.

Figaro is great!
I am great, the greatest; and really very
fortunate!
Day and night, I'm ready to do everything,
always busy, always on the go.

Of a thousand professions, that of a barber
is the most noble.
Razors, bibs, lancets and scissors are
always ready at my command.

The resources of my trade are for the
young lady as well as for the cavalier.
What a great life, what pleasures an
excellent barber has!

Everyone calls for me, everyone wants me:
women, men, old and young.
A wig here, a quick shave there,
some medicine here, deliver a letter there.

Figaro, Figaro!
I'm here, I'm here.
Figaro, Figaro!
I'm coming.
What clamor!
What people!

For heaven's sake, one at a time!
Ever ready like lightning:
I am the city's factotum.
Oh, great Figaro!
You're great, the greatest;
for you, fortune is waiting.

Figaro continues to pride his talents and good fortune.

FIGARO:
Ah, ah! Che bella vita!
Faticar poco, divertirsi assai,
e in tasca sempre aver qualche doblone
gran frutto della mia riputazione.
Ecco qua: senza Figaro non si accasa in
Siviglia una ragazza: a me la vedovella
ricorre pel marito:

FIGARO:
Oh, what a beautiful life!
I tire little and enjoy myself much,
and money is always in my pocket,
a big reward for my reputation.
Here I am. Without Figaro a young girl
cannot marry in Seville, and a widow
cannot find a new husband.

io, colla scusa del pettine di giorno,
della chitarra col favor la notte,
a tutti onestamente, non fo per dir,
m'adatto a far piacere.
Oh che vita, che vita! Oh che mestiere!
Orsù, presto a bottega.

For favors, I use the pretext of my comb by
day, and my guitar in the evening.
I am honest with everyone, I don't offend,
and I am always pleasant.
What a life! What a profession!
Now, off to the emporium.

CONTE:
(È desso, o pur m'inganno?)

COUNT: *(emerging from hiding)*
(It is him, or am I imagining?)

FIGARO:
(Chi sarà mai costui?)

FIGARO:
(Now who can that be?)

CONTE:
(Oh, è lui senz'altro!)
Figaro!

COUNT:
(I'm definitely not mistaken!)
Figaro!

FIGARO:
Mio padrone
Oh, chi veggo! Eccellenza!

FIGARO: *(recognizing the Count)*
My lord. Whom do I see!
It's your Excellency!

CONTE:
Zitto, zitto, prudenza!
Qui non son conosciuto,
nè vo' farmi conoscere.
Per questo ho le mie gran ragioni.

COUNT:
Quiet, be careful!
No one knows me here,
and I don't want to be recognized.
I have good reasons for this request.

FIGARO:
Intendo, intendo, la lascio in libertà.

FIGARO:
I understand, I'll leave you alone.

CONTE:
No.

COUNT:
No, stay here.

FIGARO:
Che serve?

FIGARO:
For what reason?

CONTE:
No, dico: resta qua; (forse ai disegni miei
non giungi inopportuno.) Ma cospetto!
Dimmi un po', buona lana come ti trovo
qua? Poter del mondo!
Ti veggo grasso e tondo.

COUNT:
Stay here and I'll tell you. .(Perhaps the
timing of my plans is opportune.) By the
way, tell me my friend, how come I have
found you here? Of all places in the world!
I see you've put on some weight.

FIGARO:
La miseria, signore!

FIGARO:
That's from suffering, my lord!

CONTE:
Ah birbo!

COUNT:
You rascal!

FIGARO:
Grazie.

FIGARO:
Thank you.

CONTE:
Hai messo ancor giudizio?

COUNT:
Have you behaved yourself?

FIGARO:
Oh! E come.
Ed ella, come in Siviglia?

FIGARO:
Of course, as always.
But tell me why you're in Seville?

CONTE:
Or te lo spiego. Al Prado vidi un fior di
bellezza, una fanciulla figlia d'un certo
medico barbogio che qua da pochi di' s'è
stabilito.
Io, di questa invaghito, lasciai patria e
parenti, e qua men venni.
E qua la notte e il giorno passo girando a
que' balconi intorno.

COUNT:
I'll explain. I saw a beautiful young lady on
the Prado, the daughter of a senile old
doctor, who a few days ago, moved into
this house.
Because I'm enamored by her charm, I left
home and family and came here.
Night and stay I come her and wait under
this balcony.

FIGARO:
A que' balconi? Un medico? Oh cospetto!
Siete ben fortunato;
sui maccheroni il cacio v'è cascato.

FIGARO:
Beneath this balcony? A doctor?
By the way, you're indeed very fortunate;
your hunted pigeon can be caught.

CONTE:
Come?

COUNT:
Explain?

FIGARO:
Certo. Là dentro io son barbiere,
parrucchier, chirurgo, botanico, spezial,
veterinario, il faccendier di casa.

FIGARO:
Certainly. I do everything in that house. I
am barber, hairdresser, surgeon, herbalist,
chemist, and veterinarian.

CONTE:
Oh che sorte!

COUNT:
What luck!

FIGARO:
Non basta. La ragazza figlia non è del
medico. È soltanto la sua pupilla!

FIGARO:
And that's not all. The young girl is not the
doctor's daughter, she's only his ward.

CONTE:
Oh, che consolazione!

COUNT:
Ph, what a consolation!

FIGARO:
Perciò? Zitto!

FIGARO:
How so? Quiet!

CONTE:
Cos' è?

COUNT:
Why?

FIGARO:
S'apre il balcone.

FIGARO:
The balcony door is opening.

Figaro and the Count hide as Rosina comes out on the balcony.

ROSINA:
Non è venuto ancor. Forse...

ROSINA:
He hasn't come yet. Perhaps...

CONTE:
Oh, mia vita! Mio nume! Mio tesoro!
Vi veggo alfine, alfine.

COUNT:
Oh, my life! My goddess! My treasure!
Finally, I see her.

ROSINA:
Oh, che vergogna!
Vorrei dargli il biglietto.

ROSINA: *(holding a letter)*
What a shame!
I wanted to give him the letter.

BARTOLO:
Ebben, ragazza?
Il tempo è buono.
Cos'è quella carta?

BARTOLO: *(appearing on the balcony)*
Well girl, what is it?
It is a beautiful day.
What is that letter?

ROSINA:
Niente, niente, signor: son le parole
dell'aria dell'Inutil Precauzione.

ROSINA:
Nothing, sir. They are words from an aria
from The Vain Precaution.

CONTE:
Ma brava dell'Inutil Precauzione.

COUNT:
How terrific, from The Vain Precaution.

FIGARO:
Che furba!

FIGARO:
She's cunning!

BARTOLO:
Cos'è questa Inutil Precauzione?

BARTOLO:
What is this Vain Precaution?

ROSINA:
Oh, bella! È il titolo del nuovo dramma in
musica.

ROSINA:
It's beautiful! It's the title of a new drama
with music.

BARTOLO:
Un dramma! Bella cosa! Sarà al solito
un dramma semiserio, un lungo,
malinconico, noioso, poetico strambotto!
Barbaro gusto! Secolo corrotto!

BARTOLO:
A drama! Beautiful! These days there's
only tragicomedy. They're long,
nonsensical, noisy, and poetically eccentric!
Barbarous taste in a corrupt century!

ROSINA:
Oh, me meschina! L'aria m'è caduta.
Raccoglietela presto.

ROSINA: *(letting the letter fall)*
How unfortunate! The aria has fallen.
Could you please get it quickly.

BARTOLO:
Vado, vado.

BARTOLO:
I'm going right away.

ROSINA:
Ps! Ps!

ROSINA: *(calling the Count)*
Psst! Psst!

CONTE:
T'ho inteso.

COUNT: *(as he grabs the letter)*
I hear you.

ROSINA:
Presto.

ROSINA:
Hurry.

CONTE:
Non temete.

COUNT: *(as he hides the letter)*
Don't worry.

BARTOLO:
Son qua. Dov'è?

BARTOLO: *(looking for the letter)*
I'm here. Where is it?

ROSINA:
Ah, il vento l'ha portata via. Guardate.

ROSINA: *(from the balcony)*
The wind blew it away. Look again.

BARTOLO:
Io non la veggo.
Eh, signorina, non vorrei...
(Cospetto! Costei m'avesse preso!)
In casa, in casa, animo, su! A chi dico?
In casa, presto.

BARTOLO:
I don't see it.
Young lady, I don't...
(I've suspicions that she's fooling me!)
Go inside the house, my love! Whom were
you talking to? Inside, quickly.

ROSINA:
Vado, vado. Che furia!

ROSINA:
I'm going. What anger!

BARTOLO:
Quel balcone io voglio far murare.
Dentro, dico.

BARTOLO:
I'm going to clone in that balcony.
I'm telling you to go inside.

ROSINA:
Ah, che vita da crepare!

ROSINA:
What a life of torment!

As Rosina retires from the balcony, Bartolo reenters the house.

CONTE:
Povera disgraziata!
Il suo stato infelice sempre più m'interessa.

COUNT:
That poor mistreated young girl!
Her unhappy situation arouses my interest
even

FIGARO:
Presto, presto: vediamo cosa scrive.

FIGARO:
Quickly, let's see what she has written.

CONTE:
Appunto. Leggi.

COUNT:
Right. You read it.

FIGARO:
"Le vostre assidue premure hanno eccitata la
mia curiosità. Il mio tutore è per uscir di casa;
appena si sarà allontanato, procurate con
qualche mezzo ingegnoso d'indicarmi
il vostro nome, il vostro stato e le vostre
intenzioni. Io non posso giammai comparire
al balcone senza l'indivisibile compagnia del
mio tiranno. Siate però certo che tutto è
disposta a fare, per rompere le sue catene....
la sventurata Rosina."

FIGARO: *(reading the letter)*
"Your earnest attentions have excited my
curiosity. My guardian is leaving the
house. As soon as he is far away, figure out
some way to let me know your name, your
background, and your intentions. I can
never appear on the balcony without my
inevitable tyrant. Be assured, however, that
I will make every effort to break the
chains....
the unfortunate Rosina."

CONTE:
Sì, sì, le romperà! Su, dimmi un poco:
che razza d'uomo è questo suo tutore?

COUNT:
Yes, she'll break the chains! Now tell me,
what kind of man is this guardian?

FIGARO:
È un vecchio indemoniato, avaro,
sospettoso, brontolone; avrà cent'anni
indosso e vuol fare il galante.
Indovinate! Per mangiare a Rosina
tutta l'eredità, s'è fitto in capo di volerla
sposare. Aiuto!

FIGARO:
He's an old demon, stingy, suspicious, and
a grumbler. He's like a hundred years old,
but he thinks he's a gallant.
Just imagine! He'll devour Rosina and all
her inheritance; that's why he's made his
mind up to marry her. Watch out!

CONTE:
Che?

COUNT:
What?

FIGARO:
S'apre la porta.

FIGARO:
The door of the house is opening.

The Count and Figaro quickly hide as Bartolo exits the house,
brusquely barking orders to his servants as he departs.

BARTOLO:
Fra momenti io torno; non aprite a nessun.
Se Don Basilio venisse a ricercarmi, che
m'aspetti. Le mie nozze con lei meglio è
affrettare.
Sì, dentr'oggi finir vo' quest'affare.

BARTOLO:
I'll return in a few moments; don't open
the door for anyone. If Don Basilio comes
looking for me, have him wait. I want to
take care of my marriage plans right away.
Afterwards, she can do what she wants.

Bartolo disappears in the square.

CONTE:
Dentr'oggi le sue nozze con Rosina!
Ah, vecchio rimbambito!
Ma dimmi or tu! Chi è questo Don Basilio?

COUNT:
He'll marry Rosina today!
That old dotard!
But tell me! Who is this Don Basilio?

FIGARO:
È un solenne imbroglion di matrimoni,
un collo torto, un vero disperato,
sempre senza un quattrino.
Già, è maestro di musica;
insegna alla ragazza.

FIGARO:
He's a schemer of weddings,
a sneaking scoundrel, a true hypocrite, and
always without money.
Now he's the music-master who teaches
the young girl.

CONTE:
Bene, bene; tutto giova saper.

COUNT:
Very well, it's good to know all this..

FIGARO:
Ora pensate della bella Rosina a soddisfar
le brame.

FIGARO:
Now let's concentrate on the beautiful
Rosina and satisfy your yearnings.

CONTE:
Il nome mio non le vo' dir nè il grado;
assicurarmi vo' pria ch'ella ami me, me
solo al mondo,non le ricchezze e i titoli
del conte d'Almaviva. Ah, tu potresti.

COUNT:
I don't want to tell her my background. I
want to be sure that she truly loves me,
and not my wealth and the title of Count
Almaviva. You can help me.

FIGARO:
Io? No, signore; voi stesso dovete.

FIGARO:
Me? My lord, you can do it yourself.

CONTE:
Io stesso? E come?

COUNT:
Myself? How?

FIGARO:
Zitto. Eccoci a tiro,
osservate: perbacco, non mi sbaglio.
Dietro la gelosia sta la ragazza;
presto, presto all'assalto, niun ci vede.
In una canzonetta, così, alla buona, il tutto
spiegatele, signor.

FIGARO:
Quiet. Here's the moment.
I'm right. Look.
The girl is behind the curtains; quickly act
while no one sees us.
Sing her a pretty song, and explain to her
everything you want her to know.

CONTE:
Una canzone?

COUNT:
A song?

FIGARO:
Certo. Ecco la chitarra; presto, andiamo.

FIGARO:
Sure. Here's my guitar. Hurry, let's go.

CONTE:
Ma io?

COUNT:
But how can I?

FIGARO:
Oh che pazienza!

FIGARO:
What patience I must have!

CONTE:
Ebben, proviamo.

COUNT:
All right, let's try it.

Andante
COUNT

Se il mio nome saper voi bra-ma - te, dal mio labbro il mio nome ascoltate.

Se il mio nome saper voi bramate,
dal mio labbro il mio nome ascoltate.
Io son Lindoro
che fido v'adoro,
che sposa vi bramo,
che a nome vi chiamo,
di voi sempre parlando così,
dall'aurora al tramonto del dì.

If you yearn to know my name,
listen for it to flow from my lips.
I am Lindoro,
who faithfully adores you,
who yearns to marry you,
who calls you by name
and always speaks of his love for you,
from dawn to dusk.

ROSINA:
Segui, o caro; deh, segui così!

ROSINA:
Go on dearest, don't stop!

FIGARO:
Sentite. Ah! Che vi pare?

FIGARO:
Listen! What could be better?

CONTE:
Oh, me felice!

COUNT:
I'm so thrilled!

FIGARO:
Da bravo, a voi, seguite.

FIGARO:
It's perfect, go on.

CONTE:
L'amoroso e sincero Lindoro,
non può darvi, mia cara, un tesoro.

COUNT:
The loving and sincere Lindoro,
cannot give you treasures, my dearest.

Ricco non sono,
ma un core vi dono,
un'anima amante
che fida e costante
per voi sola sospira così
dall'aurora al tramonto del dì.

I am not rich,
but I give you my heart,
and a loving soul
that is faithful and true
and yearns only for you
from dawn to dusk.

ROSINA:
L'amorosa e sincera Rosina del suo core
Lindo...

ROSINA:
If you are so loving and sincere, Rosina and
the loving Lindo...

Rosina's voice suddenly stops, as if suddenly interrupted by someone.

CONTE:
Oh cielo!

COUNT:
What happened?

FIGARO:
Nella stanza convien dir che qualcuno
entrato sia. Ella si è ritirata.

FIGARO:
Someone must have suddenly come into
the room, and she had to leave.

CONTE: (con enfasi)
Ah cospettone!
Io già deliro avvampo! Oh, ad ogni costo
vederla io voglio, vo' parlarle.
Ah, tu, tu mi devi aiutar.

COUNT: *(vehemently)*
How awful!
My anger is being inflamed! I want to see
her and talk to her, no matter the cost.
You must help me.

FIGARO:
Ih, ih, che furia!
Sì, sì, v'aiuterò.

FIGARO:
Hey, hey, what passion!
Yes, I will help you.

CONTE:
Da bravo: entr'oggi vo' che tu m'introduca
in quella casa.
Dimmi, come farai? Via! Del tuo spirito
vediam qualche prodezza.

COUNT:
Great. I want you to get me into that house
today.
Tell me, how will you do it? Come! Let's
see some productive genius.

FIGARO:
Del mio spirito.
Bene vedrò ma in oggi

FIGARO:
My genius.
Well said, but I'll have to think about it.

CONTE:
Eh via! T'intendo.
Va là, non dubitar; di tue fatiche
largo compenso avrai.

COUNT:
Come on! I understand you.
You know that I'll pay you well for your
efforts.

FIGARO:
Davver?

FIGARO:
Really?

CONTE:
Parola.

COUNT:
It's my word.

FIGARO:
Dunque, oro a discrezione?

FIGARO:
Therefore, you'll provide me with gold?

CONTE:
Oro a bizzeffe.
Animo, via.

COUNT:
An abundance of gold.
Come on, become inspired.

FIGARO:
Son pronto. Ah, non sapete i simpatici effetti
prodigiosi che, ad appagare il mio signor
Lindoro, produce in me la dolce idea dell'oro.

FIGARO:
I am ready. My dear Lindoro, you don't
realize the gratification that the delightful
idea of gold produces in me.

Allegro maestoso
FIGARO

Al -l'i - dea   di quel   me-tal-lo   por - ten - toso,   onni   possente,

All'idea di quel metallo
portentoso, onnipossente,
un vulcano la mia mente
incomincia a diventar.

The thought of that mighty metal,
is so overpowering,
that it begins to awaken thoughts in my
mind like an erupting volcano.

CONTE:
Su, vediam di quel metallo
qualche effetto sorprendente
del vulcan della tua mente
qualche mostro singolar.

COUNT:
Let's see some surprising effect
of that metal,
some extraordinary idea from
that volcano erupting in your mind.

FIGARO:
Voi dovreste travestirvi, per esempio da
soldato.

FIGARO:
You must disguise yourself, for example, as
a soldier.

CONTE:
Da soldato?

COUNT:
As a soldier?

FIGARO:
Sì, signore.

FIGARO:
Yes, my lord.

CONTE:
Da soldato? Che si fa?

COUNT:
As a soldier? What for?

FIGARO:
Oggi arriva un reggimento.

FIGARO:
A regiment arrives here today.

CONTE:
Sì, è mio amico il Colonnello.

COUNT:
Yes, and the colonel is a friend of mine.

FIGARO:
Va benon.

FIGARO:
That's fortunate.

CONTE:
Ma e poi?

COUNT:
Why?

FIGARO:
Cospetto!
Dell'alloggio col biglietto, quella porta
s'aprirà.
Che ne dite, mio signore?
Non vi par? Non l'ho trovata?

FIGARO:
This is it!
A billeting order for a soldier will open a
door.
What do you think, my lord?
Not a bad idea, right?

CONTE:
Che invenzione prelibata!
Bravo, bravo, in verità!

COUNT:
It is an excellent idea!
Great, really just great!

FIGARO:
Piano, piano un'altra idea!
Veda l'oro cosa fa.
Ubbriaco sì, ubbriaco, mio signor, si fingerà.

FIGARO:
Softly, I have another idea!
You see how gold inspires me.
Drunk, yes, you'll pretend to be drunk.

CONTE:
Ubbriaco?

COUNT:
Drunk?

FIGARO:
Sì, signore.

FIGARO:
Yes, my lord.

CONTE:
Ubbriaco? Ma perchè?

COUNT:
Drunk? But why?

FIGARO:
Perchè d'un ch'è poco in sè.
che dal vino casca già, il tutor, credete a
me, il tutor si fiderà.

FIGARO:
Because believe me, the guardian will not
fear one who's a little tipsy, a victim of too
much wine.

A DUE:
Che invenzione prelibata!
Bravo, bravo, in verita'!

BOTH:
It's an excellent idea!
Great, really a great idea!

CONTE:
Dunque.

COUNT:
Well then.

FIGARO:
All'opra.

FIGARO:
To work.

CONTE:
Andiam.

COUNT:
Let's go.

FIGARO:
Da bravo.

FIGARO:
Perfect.

CONTE:
Vado. Oh, il meglio mi scordavo!
Dimmi un po', la tua bottega per trovarti,
dove sta?

COUNT:
I forgot the most important thing!
Tell me where your emporium is so I can
find you?

FIGARO:
La bottega? Non si sbaglia;
guardi bene; eccola là..

FIGARO:
The emporium? You can't miss it.
look carefully, it's over there.

Numero quindici a mano manca
quattro gradini, facciata bianca,
cinque parrucche nella vetrina
sopra un cartello "Pomata fina",
mostra in azzurro alla moderna,
v'è per insegna una lanterna
Là senza fallo mi troverà.

Number fifteen, on the left side, up through
the alley, four steps up is a white facade.
There are five wigs in the shop-window
above a jar of "Fine ointment" and modern
wax.
You'll see a lantern.
There's where you'll find me.

CONTE:
Ho ben capito

COUNT:
I understand perfectly.

FIGARO:
Or vada presto.

FIGARO:
Let's go, quickly.

CONTE:
Tu guarda bene.

COUNT:
Be careful.

FIGARO:
Io penso al resto.

FIGARO:
I'll take care of everything.

CONTE:
Di te mi fido.

COUNT:
I have faith in you.

FIGARO:
Colà l'attendo.

FIGARO:
Leave it all to me.

CONTE:
Mio caro Figaro.

COUNT:
My dear Figaro.

FIGARO:
Intendo, intendo.

FIGARO:
I understand.

CONTE:
Porterò meco...

COUNT:
I'll bring with me...

FIGARO:
La borsa piena.

FIGARO:
A full purse.

CONTE:
Sì, quel che vuoi, ma il resto poi.

COUNT:
Yes, you do your part, I'll do the rest.

FIGARO:
Oh non si dubiti, che bene andrò.

FIGARO:
Have no doubt, your success is assured.

Allegro
COUNT ALMAVIVA

Ah che d'a - mo - re la fiamma io sen - to,

CONTE:
Ah, che d'amore
la fiamma io sento,
nunzia di giubilo
e di contento!
D'ardore insolito
quest'alma accende,
e di me stesso
maggior mi fa.

COUNT:
Love,
I feel its flames,
tidings of joy
and contentment!
This soul rises
to unrivaled passion,
and within me,
it makes me feel wonderful.

FIGARO:
Delle monete
il suon già sento!
L'oro già viene,
viene l'argento;

FIGARO:
Already I feel the
resonance of money!
The gold already comes,
the silver comes;

eccolo, eccolo	here it is,
che in tasca scende;	and it goes into my pocket
e di me stesso	and close to me
maggior mi fa.	it make me feel wonderful.

As the Count leaves, Figaro enters Bartolo's house. Fiorello enters the square.

FIORELLO:

Evviva il mio padrone!
Due ore, ritto in piè, là come un palo
mi fa aspettare e poi mi pianta e se ne va.
Corpo di Bacco!
Brutta cosa servire un padron come questo,
nobile, giovinotto e innamorato;
questa vita, cospetto, è un gran tormento!
Ah, durarla così non me la sento!

FIORELLO:

Long live my master!
I was standing there two hours, planted
like a pole as he went his way.
Body of Bacchus!
It is hard to serve a master like this one,
noble, young, and in love;
this life is great torment!
I can't bear it anymore, and I won't!

A room in Dr. Bartolo's house. The windows and shutters are closed.
Rosina is alone, and contemplates a letter she holds in her hand.

Andante
ROSINA

U - na vo - ce po - co fa   qui   nel cor   mi ri - suono,

ROSINA:

Una voce poco fa
qui nel cor mi risuonò;
il mio cor ferito è già,
e Lindor fu che il piagò.
Sì, Lindoro mio sarà;
lo giurai, la vincerò.

Il tutor ricuserà,
io l'ingegno aguzzerò.
Alla fin s'accheterà
e contenta io resterò.
Sì, Lindoro mio sarà;
lo giurai, la vincerò.

ROSINA:

A little while ago,
a voice resounded in my heart,
my heart that is already wounded,
but Lindoro will heal it.
Yes, Lindoro will be mine;
I swear that I will triumph.

My guardian will disapprove,
so I'll sharpen my wits.
In the end, I'll be clever
and I'll be happy.
Yes, Lindoro will be mine,
I swear that I will triumph.

Io sono docile, son rispettosa,
sono obbediente, dolce, amorosa;
mi lascio reggere, mi fo guidar.
Ma se mi toccano dov'è il mio debole
sarò una vipera e cento trappole
prima di cedere farò giocar.
Sì, sì, la vincerò.

Potessi almeno mandargli questa lettera.
Ma come?
Di nessun qui mi fido;
il tutore ha cent'occhi basta, basta;
sigilliamola intanto.

Rosina goes to the desk and seals the letter.

Con Figaro, il barbier, dalla finestra
discorrer l'ho veduto più d'un'ora;
Figaro è un galantuomo, un giovin di buon
core.
Chi sa eh'ei non protegga il nostro amore.

Figaro enters.

FIGARO:
Oh buon dì, signorina!

ROSINA:
Buon giorno, signor Figaro.

FIGARO:
Ebbene, che si fa?

ROSINA:
Si muor di noia.

FIGARO:
Oh diavolo! Possibile!
Un ragazza bella e spiritosa.

ROSINA:
Ah, ah, mi fate ridere!
Che mi serve lo spirito che giova la bellezza
se chiusa io sempre sto fra quattro mura
che mi par d'esser proprio in sepoltura?

I am responsible, I am respectful,
I am obedient, gentle, loving,
I can be ruled and I can be guided.
But if you hurt me
I will be a viper with a hundred ways to
stop you and make a fool of you.
Yes, I will triumph.

I must be able to send him this letter.
But how?
I trust no one here; and it's frightful, my
guardian has a hundred eyes.
Anyway, I'll seal the letter.

I saw him this morning with Figaro, the
barber.
Figaro is a good man, a young man with a
good heart.
Who knows, perhaps he can help us!

FIGARO:
Good day, miss!

ROSINA:
Good morning, Mr. Figaro.

FIGARO:
Well, what can I do?

ROSINA:
I'm dying from anxiety.

FIGARO:
Devil! That's not possible for a girl so
beautiful and full of spirit.

ROSINA:
You make me laugh!
What good is beauty and spirit if I'm
always imprisoned between these four
walls that are like a tomb?

FIGARO:
In sepoltura? Ohibò!

Sentite io voglio

FIGARO:
A tomb? Nonsense!
(taking her aside)
I have something for you.

ROSINA:
Ecco il tutor.

ROSINA:
Here comes my guardian.

FIGARO:
Davvero?

FIGARO:
Really?

ROSINA:
Certo, certo; è il suo passo.

ROSINA:
Indeed, I hear his footsteps.

FIGARO:
Salva, salva; fra poco ci rivedrem: ho da
dirvi qualche cosa.

FIGARO:
But we'll see each other soon. I have
something to tell you.

ROSINA:
E ancor io, signor Figaro.

ROSINA:
And I have something for you.

FIGARO:
Bravissima. Vado.

FIGARO:
Great. I'm going.

Figaro hides as Dr. Bartolo approaches.

ROSINA:
Quanto è garbato!

ROSINA:
He is so charming!

BARTOLO:
Ah, disgraziato Figaro!
Ah, indegno! Ah, maledetto! Ah, scellerato!

BARTOLO:
That contemptible Figaro!
Unworthy! Damned! A rogue!

ROSINA:
(Ecco qua: sempre grida.)

ROSINA:
(He's always shouting.)

BARTOLO:
Ma si può dar di peggio!
Uno spedale ha fatto
di tutta la famiglia
a forza d'oppio, sangue e stranutiglia.
Signorina, il barbiere lo vedeste?

BARTOLO:
It couldn't be worse!
He took the entire family
and made a hospital of the house with
powerful opium, blood and anesthetics.
Miss, have you seen the barber?

ROSINA:
Perchè?

ROSINA:
Why?

BARTOLO:
Perchè lo vo' sapere.

BARTOLO:
Because I want to know.

ROSINA:
Forse anch'egli v'adombra?

ROSINA:
Perhaps he also resents you?

BARTOLO:
E perchè no?

BARTOLO:
And why should he?

ROSINA:
Ebben, ve lo dirò. Sì, l'ho veduto,
gli ho parlato, mi piace, m'è' simpatico
il suo discorso, il suo gioviale aspetto.
(Crepa di rabbia, vecchio maledetto.)

ROSINA:
Well, I'll tell you. Yes, I saw him and
I spoke to him. He's very nice to me in his
conversation and manner.
(Burst in anger you damned old man.)

Rosina leaves.

BARTOLO:
Vedete che grazietta!
Più l'amo, e più mi sprezza la briccona.
Certo, certo è il barbiere che la mette in
malizia.
Chi sa cosa le ha detto!
Chi sa! Or lo saprò.

BARTOLO:
Look at the appreciation I get!
The more I love her, the more she becomes
a rascal. The barber has certainly put her to
mischief.
Who knows what he said to her!
Who knows! I will find out.

(Bartolo calls his servants)

Ehi! Berta! Ambrogio!

Hey! Berta! Ambrosio!

Berta enters sneezing profusely.

BERTA:
Achoo!

BERTA:
Eccì!

Ambrosio enters yawning.

AMBROSIO:
Ah! che comanda?

AMBROSIO:
You called?

BARTOLO:
Dimmi.

BARTOLO:
Tell me.

BERTA:
Eccì!

BERTA:
Achoo!

BARTOLO:
Il barbiere parlato ha con Rosina?

BARTOLO:
Did the barber speak with Rosina?

BERTA:
Ecci!

BARTOLO:
Rispondi almen tu, babbuino!

AMBROSIO:
Ah, ah!

BARTOLO:
Che pazïenza!

AMBROSIO:
Ah, ah! Che sonno!

BARTOLO:
Ebben!

BERTA:
Venne, ma io...

BARTOLO:
Rosina...

AMBROSIO:
Ah!

BERTA:
Ecci!

BARTOLO:
Che serve! Eccoli qua, son mezzo morti.
Andate.

AMBROSIO:
Ah!

BERTA:
Ecci!

BARTOLO:
Eh, il diavol che vi porti!

BERTA:
Achoo!

BARTOLO:
Answer me, you baboon!

AMBROSIO: *(yawning)*
Ah, ah!

BARTOLO:
What patience I need!

AMBROSIO:
I'm so sleepy!

BARTOLO:
Well!

BERTA:
He came here, but I...

BARTOLO:
Rosina...

AMBROSIO:
Ah!

BERTA:
Achoo!

BARTOLO:
What servants! Here they are, half dead.
Go.

AMBROSIO:
Ah!

BERTA:
Achoo!

BARTOLO:
Go to the devil!

After Berta and Ambrosio leave, Don Basilio arrives.

BARTOLO:
Ah! Barbiere d'inferno tu me la pagherai!
Qua, Don Basilio; giungete a tempo!
Oh! Io voglio, per forza o per amor, dentro
domani sposar la mia Rosina. Avete inteso?

BASILIO:
Eh, voi dite benissimo e appunto io qui
veniva ad avvisarvi, ma segretezza!
È giunto il Conte d'Almaviva.

BARTOLO:
Chi? L'incognito amante della Rosina?

BASILIO:
Appunto quello.

BARTOLO:
Oh diavolo!
Ah, qui ci vuol rimedio!

BASILIO:
Certo; ma alla sordina.

BARTOLO:
Sarebbe a dir?

BASILIO:
Così, con buona grazia bisogna principiare
a inventar qualche favola che al pubblico lo
metta in mala vista, che comparir lo faccia
un uomo infame, un'anima perduta.
Io, io vi servirò: fra quattro giorni,
credete a me, Basilio ve lo giura,
noi lo farem sloggiar da queste mura.

BARTOLO:
E voi credete?

BASILIO:
Oh certo! È il mio sistema.e non sbaglia.

BARTOLO:
E vorreste?
Ma una calunnia...

BARTOLO:
Damned barber, you will pay for this!
Don Basilio, you've arrived just in time!
Either by force or love, I want to marry
Rosina tomorrow. You understand me?

BASILIO: *(bowing reverently)*
Well said, and the reason I came here is to
advise you of something very confidential!
Count Almaviva has arrived in town.

BARTOLO:
Who? Is he Rosina's unknown lover?

BASILIO:
I believe so.

BARTOLO:
The devil!
We have to remedy the situation!

BASILIO:
Certainly, but secretly.

BARTOLO:
What do you mean?

BASILIO:
With all respect one needs to invent some
story that will disgrace him in the eyes of
the public, and make him appear as a man
of dishonor, a lost soul.
I will help you. Believe me, Basilio swears
to you that within four days, we will drive
him out of this city.

BARTOLO:
You believe you can do this?

BASILIO:
Certainly! My system never fails.

BARTOLO:
And that's what you want to do?
But slander...

BASILIO:
Ah, dunque la calunnia cos'è voi non sapete?

BASILIO:
But don't you understand what slander is?

BARTOLO:
No, davvero.

BARTOLO:
No, not really.

BASILIO:
No? Uditemi e tacete.

BASILIO:
No? Than listen to me and be quiet.

Allegro
BASILIO

La   -   ca - lunnia   e un ven - ti - cel - lo,

La calunnia è un venticello,
un'auretta assai gentile
che insensibile, sottile,
leggermente, dolcemente
incomincia a sussurrar.

Slander is a light wind,
a zephyr so gentle
that imperceptibly, finely,
lightly, gently,
it begins to murmur.

Piano piano, terra terra,
sottovoce, sibilando,
va scorrendo, va ronzando;
nelle orecchie della gente
s'introduce destramente
e le teste ed i cervelli
fa stordire e fa gonfiar.

Softly, softly, it lands,
faintly, hissing,
it begins to flow and burn;
suspicion is introduced into
the ears of the people
and the head and brains
become dazed and inflated.

Dalla bocca fuori uscendo
lo schiamazzo va crescendo
prende forza a poco a poco,
vola già di loco in loco;
sembra il tuono, la tempesta
che nel sen della foresta
va fischiando, brontolando
e ti fa d'orror gelar.

From the open mouth, the clamor begins to
increase little by little
increasing in force,
and flying from place to place;
The sound is like a storm in the
heart of the forest
that is whistling and grumbling
and causing horrifying chills.

Alla fin trabocca e scoppia,
si propaga, si raddoppia
e produce un'esplosione
come un colpo di cannone,
un tremuoto, un temporale,
un tumulto generale,
che fa l'aria rimbombar.

Finally it overflows and bursts,
multiplying itself,
and producing an explosion
like the shot from a canon,
a tremor, a storm,
a total confusion,
that makes the air thunder.

E il meschino calunniato,
avvilito, calpestato,
sotto il pubblico flagello
per gran sorte ha crepar.

The miserable slandered one,
vilified, tramped upon,
and under the public scourge,
has been fated to destruction.

Ah! Che ne dite?

What is your opinion?

BARTOLO:
Eh! Sarà ver, ma intanto
si perde tempo e qui stringe il bisogno.
No: vo' fare a mio modo:
in mia camera andiam.
Voglio che insieme il contratto di nozze ora
stendiamo.
Quando sarà mia moglie, da questi
zerbinotti innamorati metterla in salvo sara'
pensier mio.

BARTOLO:
It's good, but meanwhile we don't have
time, and our needs are pressing.
No, I want to do it my own way: come with
me to my room.
Together, let's draw up the marriage
contract right away..
After she is my wife, I'll put a stop to her
flirtations with dandies, and she'll respond
to my wishes.

BASILIO:
(Vengan denari: al resto son qua io.)

BASILIO:
(Let the money come: and I'll do the rest.)

After Bartolo and Basilio leave, Figaro cautiously emerges from hiding.

FIGARO:
Ma bravi! ma benone!
Ho inteso tutto. Evviva il buon dottore!
Povero babbuino!
Tua sposa? Eh via pulisciti il bocchino.
Or che stan là chiusi,
procuriam di parlare alla ragazza:
eccola appunto.

FIGARO:
How wonderful! What luck!
I overheard everything. Long live the good
doctor! That poor baboon!
Your wife? Go and clean your mouth.
Or else leave it closed.
I must find Rosina right away, and tell her
and warn her. Appropo, there she is.

Rosina enters.

ROSINA:
Ebbene, signor Figaro.

ROSINA:
Well, Mr. Figaro.

FIGARO:
Gran cose, signorina.

FIGARO:
Very important news, little lady.

ROSINA:
Si, davvero?

ROSINA:
Really?

FIGARO:
Mangerem dei confetti.

FIGARO:
We'll be eating wedding cake soon.

ROSINA:
Come sarebbe a dir?

FIGARO:
Sarebbe a dire che il vostro bel tutore ha
stabilito esser dentro doman vostro marito.

ROSINA:
Eh, via!

FIGARO:
Oh, ve lo giuro; a stender il contratto
col maestro di musica la' dentro or s'è
serrato.

ROSINA:
Sì? oh, l'ha sbagliata affè!
Povero sciocco! L'avrà a far con me.
Ma dite, signor Figaro,
voi poco fa sotto le mie finestre
parlavate a un signore

FIGARO:
Ah, un mio cugino, un bravo giovinotto;
buona testa, ottimo cuor; qui venne
i suoi studi a compire e il poverin cerca di
far fortuna.

ROSINA:
Fortuna? Oh, la farà.

FIGARO:
Oh, ne dubito assai: in confidenza
ha un gran difetto addosso.

ROSINA:
Un gran difetto

FIGARO:
Ah, grande: è innamorato morto.

ROSINA:
Sì, davvero? Quel giovane, vedete
m'interessa moltissimo.

ROSINA:
What do you mean?

FIGARO:
I mean that your precious guardian has
decided to marry you tomorrow.

ROSINA:
Nonsense!

FIGARO:
I swear it; he's there in the closed room
with the music teacher drawing up the
contract.

ROSINA:
Really? That's what they're doing!
Poor fools! They'll have to contend with me.
But listen, Figaro, a little while ago you
were under my window talking with a
gentleman.

FIGARO:
Oh, my cousin, a promising young man;
very smart, and a good heart. He came
here to complete his studies and then make
his fortune.

ROSINA:
Fortune? Oh, he will make it.

FIGARO:
I doubt it. I'll tell you confidentially, he has
a big problem.

ROSINA:
A big problem. .

FIGARO:
Yes, big, he's fatally in love.

ROSINA:
Really? You see, that young man interests
me very much.

FIGARO:
Per bacco!

ROSINA:
Non mi credete?

FIGARO:
Oh sì!

ROSINA:
E la sua bella, dite, abita lontano?

FIGARO:
Qui! Due passi.

ROSINA:
Ma è bella?

FIGARO:
Oh, bella assai!
Eccovi il suo ritratto in due parole:
grassotta, genialotta,
capello nero, guancia porporina,
occhio che parla, mano che innamora

ROSINA:
E il nome?

FIGARO:
Ah, il nome ancora?
Il nome Ah, che bel nome!
Si chiama...

ROSINA:
Ebbene, si chiama?

FIGARO:
Si chiama R, o, Ro, s, i, si,
Rosi, n, a, na, Rosina!

ROSINA:
Dunque io son tu non m'inganni?
Dunque io son la fortunata!
(Già me l'ero immaginata:
lo sapeva pria di te.)

FIGARO:
Really!

ROSINA:
You don't believe me?

FIGARO:
Oh, I do!

ROSINA:
Tell me, does his beloved live far away?

FIGARO:
Here! Close by.

ROSINA:
Is she pretty?

FIGARO:
Very pretty!
Let me describe her in a few words:
round and dimpled, pleasant,
dark hair, rosy cheeks,
expressive eyes, and a loving hand.

ROSINA:
And what is her name?

FIGARO:
You want her name too?
It is such a beautiful name!
Her name is...

ROSINA:
Well? What is her name?

FIGARO:
Her name is R, o, Ro, s, i, si,
Rosi, n, a, na, Rosina!

ROSINA:
Can I be sure you're not deceiving me?
Then I am the fortunate one!
(I knew I wasn't imagining; I knew he was
the hero I dreamed of.)

FIGARO:
Di Lindoro il vago oggetto siete voi, bella
Rosina.
(Oh, che volpe sopraffina,
ma l'avrà da far con me.)

FIGARO:
Beautiful Rosina, you are the desired object
of Lindoro's love.
(The fox is cunning, but she will get
nothing more from me.)

ROSINA:
Senti, senti ma a Lindoro per parlar come si
fà?

ROSINA:
Listen, tell me how I'll be able to talk to
Lindoro?

FIGARO:
Zitto, zitto, qui Lindoro per parlarvi or or
sarà.

FIGARO:
Take it easy. Lindoro will be coming here to
talk to you.,

ROSINA:
Per parlarmi? Bravo! Bbravo!
Venga pur, ma con prudenza;
io già moro d'impazienza!
Ma che tarda? Ma che fa?

ROSINA:
To talk to me? Great! Wonderful!
Tell him to be cautious;
I'm already dying from impatience!
What's keeping him? What is he doing?

FIGARO:
Egli attende qualche segno, poverin, del
vostro affetto; sol due righe di biglietto
gli mandate, e qui verrà.
Che ne dite?

FIGARO:
The poor boy is waiting for some sign of
your affection; just send him a few lines in
a letter and he'll be here.
What do you think?

ROSINA:
Non vorrei

ROSINA:
I can't.

FIGARO:
Su, coraggio.

FIGARO:
Be brave.

ROSINA:
Non saprei

ROSINA:
You don't understand.

FIGARO:
Sol due righe.

FIGARO:
Just two lines.

ROSINA:
Mi vergogno.

ROSINA:
I'm ashamed.

FIGARO:
Ma di che? Di che? Si sa!

FIGARO:
Why? Of what? You know!

Presto, presto; qua un biglietto.

Quickly, write a letter.

Surprising Figaro, Rosina takes a letter from her pocket and gives it to him.

ROSINA:
Un biglietto? Eccolo qua.

ROSINA:
A letter? Here it is!

FIGARO:
Già era scritto? Ve', che bestia!
Il maestro faccio a lei!
Ah, che in cattedra costei di malizia può dettar.
Donne, donne, eterni Dei, chi vi arriva a indovinar?

FIGARO: *(astonished)*
It was already written? What a fool I am!
The maestro can learn from her!
What malicious cunning she is capable of creating.
Women, eternal Gods, who can figure them out?

ROSINA:
Fortunati affetti miei!
Io comincio a respirar.
Ah, tu solo, amor, tu sei
che mi devi consolar!

ROSINA:
I am so fortunate!
I'm beginning to breathe.
You alone are the one, my love,
who has eased my heart!

Figaro departs with Rosina's letter.

ROSINA:
Ora mi sento meglio.
Questo Figaro è un bravo giovinotto.

ROSINA:
Now I feel better.
This Figaro is a good man.

Bartolo enters.

BARTOLO:
Insomma, colle buone, potrei sapere dalla mia Rosina.
Che venne a far colui questa mattina?

BARTOLO:
Come here my good child, there's something I want to ask you.
Who was here with you this morning?

ROSINA:
Figaro? Non so nulla.

ROSINA:
Figaro? Nobody else.

BARTOLO:
Ti parlò?

BARTOLO:
Did he talk you?

ROSINA:
Mi parlò.

ROSINA:
He talked to me.

BARTOLO:
Che ti diceva?

BARTOLO:
What did he say to you?

ROSINA:
Oh mi parlò di certe bagattelle del figurin di
Francia, del mal della sua figlia Marcellina.

ROSINA:
He talked to me about trifles, about French
fashions, and his daughter Marcellina's illness.

BARTOLO:
Davvero! Ed io scommetto che portò la
risposta al tuo biglietto.

BARTOLO:
Really! And I'll bet that he brought the
answer to your letter.

ROSINA:
Qual biglietto?

ROSINA:
What letter?

BARTOLO:
Che serve! L'arietta dell'Inutil Precauzione
che ti cadde staman giù dal balcone.

Vi fate rossa? (Avessi indovinato!)
Che vuol dir questo dito così sporco
d'inchiostro?

BARTOLO:
What patronizing! The aria from The Vain
Precaution that you let fall from the
balcony this morning.
You're blushing? (I must have guessed
right!) How do you explain that ink stain
on your finger?

ROSINA:
Sporco? Oh, nulla.
Io me l'avea scottato e coll'inchiostro or or
l'ho medicato.

ROSINA:
Ink? Oh, that's nothing.
I burned it and medicated it right away
with ink.

BARTOLO:
(Diavolo!) E questi fogli
Or son cinque eran sei.

BARTOLO:
(Devil!) And these sheets of paper.
There are now only five, and there were six.

ROSINA:
Que' fogli? È vero.
D'uno mi son servita a mandar dei confetti
a Marcellina.

ROSINA:
Those papers? Right. .
I used one sheet to wrap some candy for
Marcellina.

BARTOLO:
Bravissima! E la penna perchè fu temperata?

BARTOLO:
Good! And why is the pen filled with ink?

ROSINA:
(Maledetto!) La penna!
Per disegnare un fiore sul tamburo.

ROSINA:
(Damn it!) The pen!
To design a flower for embroidery.

BARTOLO:
Un fiore?

BARTOLO:
A flower?

ROSINA:
Un fiore.

ROSINA:
A flower.

BARTOLO:
Un fiore. Ah! Fraschetta!

BARTOLO:
A flower. You cunning one!

ROSINA:
Davver.

ROSINA:
It's true.

BARTOLO:
Zitta!

BARTOLO:
Quiet!

ROSINA:
Credete.

ROSINA:
Believe me.

BARTOLO:
Basta così.

BARTOLO:
That's enough.

ROSINA:
Signor...

ROSINA:
Sir...

BARTOLO:
Non più, tacete!

BARTOLO:
No more, be quiet!

Andante maestoso
BARTOLO

A un dottor della mia sorte queste scu - se,si gnori - na!

A un dottor della mia sorte
queste scuse, signorina!
Vi consiglio, mia carina,
un po' meglio a imposturar.
I confetti alla ragazza!
Il ricamo sul tamburo!
Vi scottaste: eh via! Eh via!

To a doctor of my stature,
you dare offer such excuses, young lady!
I advise you, my dear,
to use a better deception.
Candy for the girl!
Design for embroidery!
Burned your finger. Nonsense!

Ci vuol altro, figlia mia,
per potermi corbellar.
Perchè manca là quel foglio?
Vo' saper cotesto imbroglio.
Sono inutili le smorfie;
ferma là, non mi toccate!

You need a better explanation
to make me believe you.
Why is a paper missing?
I want to get to the bottom of this.
Your grimaces are useless,
stop there, and stop playing with me!

Figlia mia non lo sperate
ch'io mi lasci infinocchiar.
Via, carina, confessate;
son disposto a perdonar.

Don't continue to hope
that I'm going to let you go on lying.
Come on, my dear, confess;
I'm ready to pardon you.

Non parlate? Vi ostinate?

You don't talk? Why are you so obstinate?

So ben io quel che ho da far.
Signorina, un'altra volta
quando Bartolo andrà fuori,
la consegna ai servitori a suo modo far
saprà.

I know well what I have to do.
Young lady, the next time
that Bartolo goes out of the house,
I will order the servants to keep you locked
inside.

Ah, non servono le smorfie,
faccia pur la gatta morta.
Cospetton! Per quella porta
nemmen l'aria entrar potrà.
E Rosina innocentina,
sconsolata, disperata,
in sua camera serrata
fin ch'io voglio star dovrà.

Don't feed me lies,
or you'll become a dead cat.
Besides! Through that door,
not even air will be able to enter.
And innocent Rosina,
disconsolate, desperate,
I will lock you in your room,
until I choose to let you out.

Bartolo exits.

ROSINA:
Brontola quanto vuoi,
chiudi porte e finestre.
Io me ne rido: già di noi femmine alla più
marmotta per aguzzar l'ingegno e far la
spiritosa, tutto a un tratto, basta chiuder la
chiave e il colpo è fatto.

ROSINA:
You grumble so much about
closing doors and windows.
It makes me laugh: women are like
woodchucks. They know how to sharpen
their wits and spirits; and tighten their hold
on their prey and strike.

As Rosina exits, Berta enters.

BERTA:
Finora in questa camera mi parve di sentir
un mormorio;
sarà stato il tutor, colla pupilla non ha
un'ora di ben.
Queste ragazze non la voglion capir.

BERTA:
Just before, I thought I heard murmuring in
this room;
it must have been the guardian, who never
has a peaceful hour with his ward.
These girls will never learn..

Bertha hears a loud knock at the door.

Battono.

Someone's knocking.

CONTE:
Aprite.

COUNT:
Open up.

BERTA:
Vengo! Ecci! Ancora dura;
quel tabacco m'ha posta in sepoltura.

BERTA:
I'm coming! It doesn't stop. That tobacco
smell here will put me in my tomb.

Berta opens the door to the Count, disguised as a soldier.

CONTE:
Ehi di casa, buona gente!
Ehi di casa, niun mi sente!

COUNT:
Hey, in there, good people!
Hey, in there, no one hears me!

BARTOLO:
Chi è costui? Che brutta faccia!
È ubbriaco! Chi sarà?

BARTOLO:
Who can this be? What an ugly face!
He's drunk! Who are you?

CONTE:
Ehi, di casa! maledetti!

COUNT:
Hey, in there! Damned ones!

BARTOLO:
Cosa vuol, signor soldato?

BARTOLO:
What do you want, soldier?

CONTE:
Ah! Sì sì, bene obbligato.

COUNT: *(searching his pockets)*
Yes, much obliged.

BARTOLO:
(Qui costui che mai vorrà?)

BARTOLO:
(Who knows what he wants?)

CONTE:
Siete voi, aspetta un poco,
siete voi dottor Balordo?

COUNT:
You are, wait a minute,
you are Doctor Barlordo?

BARTOLO:
Che balordo?

BARTOLO:
What Balordo?

CONTE:
Ah, ah, Bertoldo?

COUNT: *(reading)*
Oh, Bertoldo?

BARTOLO:
Che Bertoldo? Eh, andate al diavolo!
Dottor Bartolo.

BARTOLO:
What Bertoldo? Go to the devil!
Doctor Bartolo.

CONTE:
Ah, bravissimo; dottor barbaro; benissimo,
già v'è poca differenza.
(Non si vede! Che impazienza!
Quanto tarda! Dove sta?)

COUNT:
Ah, very good, Doctor Barbaro; perfect,
but it's all the same.
(I don't see her! I'm so impatient!
She's late! Where is she?)

BARTOLO:
Un corno!
(Io già perdo la pazienza, qui prudenza ci
vorrà.)

BARTOLO:
What a numbskull!
(I've already lost patience, but I'll have to
be prudent.)

CONTE:
Dunque voi siete dottore?

COUNT:
So you are a doctor?

BARTOLO:
Son dottore sì, signore.

BARTOLO:
Yes, sir, I am a doctor.

CONTE:
Ah, benissimo; un abbraccio, qua, collega.

COUNT:
Wonderful, let's embrace since we are
colleagues.

BARTOLO:
Indietro!

BARTOLO:
Get back!

CONTE:
Qua.
Sono anch'io dottor per cento,
maniscalco al reggimento.

COUNT: *(forcefully embracing him)*
Here.
I am also a doctor by profession.
I am the horseshoer for the regiment.

(He presents a paper to Bartolo)

Dell'alloggio sul biglietto
osservate, eccolo qua.

Look at the paper. Here is where I am to be
billeted.

BARTOLO:
Dalla rabbia e dal dispetto io già crepo in
verità.
Ah, ch'io fo, se mi ci metto, qualche gran
bestialità!

BARTOLO:
I'm ready to die in anger from his
haughtiness.
A man of my moderation doesn't know
how to deal with such a brute!

Bartolo reads the letter.

CONTE:
(Ah, venisse il caro oggetto della mia
felicità!)
Vieni, vieni; il tuo diletto pien d'amor
t'attendo qua.)

COUNT:
(I wish that dear object of my happiness
would come!)
Come, my beloved, I await you here, full of
love for you.)

Rosina enters, shocked at the sight of the drunken soldier.

ROSINA:
Un soldato ed il tutore!
Cosa mai faranno qua?

ROSINA:
A soldier and my guardian!
What are they doing here?

CONTE:
(È Rosina; or son contento.)

COUNT:
(It is Rosina, now I'm happy.)

ROSINA:
(Ei mi guarda, e s'avvicina.)

ROSINA:
(He's staring at me, and approaches me.)

CONTE:
(Son Lindoro.)

COUNT: *(whispering to Rosina)*
(I am Lindoro.)

ROSINA:
(Oh ciel! Che sento!
Ah, giudizio, per pietà!)

ROSINA:
(Oh Heavens! What am I hearing!
Be prudent, please!)

BARTOLO:
Signorina, che cercate?
Presto, presto, andate via.

BARTOLO: *(seeing Rosina)*
Young lady, what are you looking for?
Quickly, go away.

ROSINA:
Vado, vado, non gridate.

ROSINA:
I'm going, stop shouting.

BARTOLO:
Presto, presto, via di qua.

BARTOLO:
Quickly, away from here.

CONTE:
Ehi, ragazza, vengo anch'io.

COUNT:
Hey, girl, I'm going with you.

BARTOLO:
Dove, dove, signor mio?

BARTOLO:
Where to, sir?

CONTE:
In caserma, oh, questa è bella!

COUNT:
To my quarters, oh she is so beautiful!

BARTOLO:
In caserma? Bagattella!

BARTOLO:
To your quarters? This is too much!

CONTE:
Cara!

COUNT:
My dearest!

ROSINA:
Aiuto!

ROSINA:
Help!

BARTOLO:
Olà, cospetto!

BARTOLO:
Hey, watch it!

CONTE:
Dunque vado.

COUNT:
Then, I'm going.

BARTOLO:
Oh, no, signore, qui d'alloggio non può star.

BARTOLO: *(restraining him)*
Sir, you can't lodge here.

CONTE:
Come? Come?

COUNT:
Why?

BARTOLO:
Eh, non v'è replica: ho il brevetto
d'esenzione.

BARTOLO:
This isn't an argument: I have a letter of
exemption.

CONTE:
Il brevetto?

COUNT: *(angrily)*
A letter of exemption?

BARTOLO:
Mio padrone, un momento e il mostrerò.

BARTOLO:
Sir, one moment and I'll show it you.

Bartolo goes to his desk to search for the exemption.

CONTE:
(Ah, se qui restar non posso, deh, prendete.)

COUNT: *(giving Rosina a letter)*
(In case I can't stay here any more, here,
take this.)

ROSINA:
(Ohimè, ci guarda!)

ROSINA:
(He's looking at us!)

CONTE E ROSINA:
(Cento smanie io sento addosso.
Ah, più reggere non so.)

COUNT and ROSINA:
(I feel the pangs of a hundred yearnings.
I can't take it any more.)

BARTOLO:
(Ah, trovarlo ancor non posso; ma sì, sì, lo
troverò.)

BARTOLO: *(searching the desk)*
(I can't find it right now; but I hope to find
it soon.)

Ecco qui.

Here it is.

"Con la presente il Dottor Bartolo, etcetera.
Esentiamo"

"With this letter, Doctor Bartolo,
etcetera...is exempted."

CONTE:
Eh, andate al diavolo!
Non mi state più a seccar.

COUNT: *(tosses the document away)*
Oh, go to the devil!
Don't bother me any more.

BARTOLO:
Cosa fa, signor mio caro?

BARTOLO:
What happened, my dear sir?

CONTE:
Zitto là, Dottor somaro.

COUNT:
Quiet over there, Doctor donkey.

Il mio alloggio è qui fissato e in alloggio qui vo' star.

My lodging is fixed here, and here is where I will stay.

BARTOLO:
Vuol restar?

BARTOLO:
You want to stay?

CONTE:
Restar, sicuro.

COUNT:
Sure, I will stay.

BARTOLO:
Oh, son stufo, mio padrone; presto fuori, o un buon bastone lo farà di qua sloggiar.

BARTOLO: *(holding a stick)*
I'm all heated up, officer, out of here quickly, or I'll evict you with the stick.

CONTE:
Dunque lei lei vuol battaglia?
Ben! Battaglia le vo' dar.
Bella cosa è una battaglia!
Ve la voglio qui mostrar.

COUNT:
Then you want to fight with me?
Good! I'll give you battle.
Combat is a beautiful thing!
I'll give you a demonstration.

Osservate! Questo è il fosso
L'inimico voi sarete

Look! This is the trench.
You are the enemy.

The Count thrusts his sword at Bartolo.

Attenzion

Get ready.

The Count drops a letter and whispers to Rosina to cover it with her handkerchief.

(Giù il fazzoletto.)

(Throw down your handkerchief.)

E gli amici stan di qua, attenzione!

And friends are ready!

BARTOLO:
Ferma, ferma!

BARTOLO:
Stop, stop!

The Count pretends that he has just caught sight of the letter, and picks it up.

CONTE:
Che cos'è? ah!

COUNT:
What is this?

BARTOLO:
Vo' vedere.

BARTOLO: *(watching him)*
I want to see that.

CONTE:
Sì, se fosse una ricetta!
Ma un biglietto, è mio dovere,
Mi dovete perdonar.

COUNT:
If it was a prescription!
But it is a letter and my responsibility.
You must pardon me.

The Count gives the letter and handkerchief to Rosina.

ROSINA:
Grazie, grazie!

ROSINA:
Thank you!

BARTOLO:
Grazie un corno!
Qua quel foglio; impertinente!

BARTOLO:
Thanks to a numbskull!
You impertinent fiend, give me that paper!

(to Rosina)
A chi dico? Presto qua.

What did I tell you? Out of here, quickly.

ROSINA:
Ma quel foglio che chiedete per azzardo
m'è cascato; è la lista del bucato.

ROSINA:
But that paper you're asking for that fell by
accident, is the laundry list.

As Bartolo tears the paper from her hand. Basilio enters, accompanied by Berta.

BARTOLO:
Ah, fraschetta! Presto qua.

BARTOLO:
Frivolous woman! Right here.

Ah, che vedo! Ho preso abbaglio!
È la lista, son di stucco!
Ah, son proprio un mammalucco!
Ah, che gran bestialità

What do I see! I've made a mistake!
It is a list, I'm confused!
I'm a real idiot!
What stupidity!

ROSINA E CONTE:
(Bravo, bravo il mammalucco che nel
sacco entrato è già.)

ROSINA and COUNT:.
(Great, the idiot has already been put into
our bag.)

BERTA:
(Non capisco, son di stucco; qualche
imbroglio qui ci sta.)

BERTA:
(I don't understand, I'm confused by the
bickering that is going on here.)

ROSINA:
Ecco qua! Sempre un'istoria;
sempre oppressa e maltrattata;
ah, che vita disperata!
Non la so più sopportar.

ROSINA: *(crying)*
That's the way! Always a drama;
I'm always oppressed and mistreated;
what a despairing life!
I can't bear it anymore.

BARTOLO:
Ah, Rosina poverina

BARTOLO:
My poor Rosina:

CONTE:
Via qua tu, cosa le hai fatto?

COUNT: *(threatening Bartolo)*
Get out of here, look what you have done?

BARTOLO:
Ah, fermate niente affatto.

BARTOLO:
Stop, nothing has happened.

CONTE:
Ah, canaglia, traditore!

COUNT: *(drawing his sword)*
Scoundrel, traitor!

TUTTI:
Via, fermatevi, signore.

ALL:
Sir, stop it.

CONTE:
Io ti voglio subissar!

COUNT:
I want to ruin him!

**TUTTI
eccetto il CONTE e ROSINA:**
Gente! Aiuto, soccorrete(mi/lo)

**ALL
except the COUNT and ROSINA:**
Everyone! Help me/him.

ROSINA:
Ma chetatevi.

ROSINA:
But be quiet.

CONTE:
Lasciatemi!

COUNT:
Leave me alone!

TUTTI:
Gente! Aiuto, per pietà!

ALL:
People! Help, for heaven's sake!

Figaro enters carrying a basin under his arms.

FIGARO:
Alto là!
Che cosa accadde signori miei?
Che chiasso è questo?
Eterni Dei!
Già sulla piazza a questo strepito
s'è radunata mezza città.

(Signor, giudizio, per carità.)

FIGARO:
What noise!
Gentlemen, what has happened?
What is this chaos?
Eternal Gods!
Half the city has gathered in the square
because of this noise.

(aside to the Count)
(Sir, please, be a little more prudent.)

BARTOLO:
Quest'è un birbante!

BARTOLO: *(pointing to the Count)*
This man is a ruffian!

CONTE:
Quest'è un briccone!

COUNT: *(pointing to Bartolo)*
He is the scoundrel!

BARTOLO:
Ah, disgraziato!

BARTOLO:
Disgraceful!

CONTE:
Ah, maledetto!

COUNT: *(with drawn sword)*
Damned you!

FIGARO:
Signor soldato porti rispetto, o questo fusto,
corpo del diavolo, or la creanza le insegnerà.
(Signore, giudizio, per carità.)

FIGARO: *(raising the basin threateningly)*
Have respect soldier, or this basin, like the
devil, will teach you some politeness.
(Sir, please, be more prudent.)

CONTE:
Brutto scimmiotto!

COUNT: *(to Bartolo)*
Ugly monkey!

BARTOLO:
Birbo malnato!

BARTOLO: *(to the Count)*
Conceited ass!

TUTTI:
Zitto, dottore.

ALL: *(to Bartolo)*
Quiet, doctor.

BARTOLO:
Voglio gridare.

BARTOLO:
I want to shout.

TUTTI:
Fermo, signore.

ALL: *(to the Count)*
Sir, stop.

CONTE:
Voglio ammazzare.

COUNT:
I want to kill him.

TUTTI:
Fate silenzio, per carità.

ALL:
Be quiet, for heaven's sake.

CONTE:
No, voglio ucciderlo, non v'è pietà.

COUNT:
No, I want to kill him, without pity.

The commotion suddenly stops when a violent knocking is heard on the street door.

TUTTI:
Zitti, che battono. Chi mai sarà?

ALL:
Quiet, who is knocking. Who can it be?

BARTOLO:
Chi è?

BARTOLO:
Who is it?

UFFICIALE:
Olà!

OFFICER:
Hello!

CORO:
La forza, aprite qua.

CHORUS: *(from outside)*
The police, open up.

TUTTI:
La forza! Oh diavolo!

ALL:
The police! My goodness!

FIGARO e BASILIO:
L'avete fatta!

FIGARO and BASILIO:
It's you fault!

CONTE e BARTOLO:
Niente paura. Venga pur qua.

COUNT and BARTOLO:
Don't worry. Come in.

TUTTI:
Quest'avventura, ah, come diavolo
mai finirà?

ALL:
How the devil will this adventure end?

An officer and soldiers enter.

CORO:
Fermi tutti. Niun si mova.
Miei signori, che si fa?
Questo chiasso d'onde è nato?
La cagione presto qua.

CHORUS:
Hold it everyone. No one move.
Gentlemen, what happened?
What's the cause of this disturbance?
The reason, right away.

BARTOLO:
Questa bestia di soldato, mio signor, m'ha
maltrattato.

BARTOLO:
Sir, this brutish soldier, has mistreated me.

FIGARO:
Io qua venni, mio signore, questo chiasso
ad acquetare.

FIGARO:
Sir, I came here, in order to quiet down the
uproar.

BERTA e BASILIO:
Fa un inferno di rumore, parla sempre
d'ammazzare.

BERTA and BASILIO:
It was an inferno of noise, with talk always
about murder.

CONTE:
In alloggio quel briccone non mi volle qui
accettare.

COUNT:
That scoundrel refused to accept me for
lodging here.

ROSINA:
Perdonate, poverino, tutto effetto fu del
vino.

ROSINA:
Pardon him, the poor man was affected by
too much wine.

UFFICIALE:
Ho inteso.
Galantuom, siete in arresto.
Fuori presto, via di qua.

OFFICIAL: *(to the Count)*
I understand.
My good man, you are under arrest.
Outside quickly, and away from here.

CONTE:
Io in arresto? Fermi, olà.

COUNT:
Me, arrested? Hold it.

*With an authoritative gesture, the Count motions the guard back, takes the Officer aside,
and shows him a paper identifying him as the Count. The Officer is astonished. He
orders the guard to retire to the back, where he places himself at the head.
All stand in shock and amazement.*

Fred - da ed im -mo-bi - le co -me un - a statu - a,

**BARTOLO, ROSINA, BASILIO e
BERTA:**
Fredd(o/a) ed immobile
come una statua
fiato non restami da respirar.

**BARTOLO, ROSINA, BASILIO and
BERTA:**
Cold and stationary
like a statue,
I can hardly breathe at all.

CONTE:
Freddo ed immobile
come una statua,
fiato non restagli da respirar.

COUNT:
Cold and stationary
like a statue,
he can hardly breathe at all.

FIGARO:
Guarda Don Bartolo!
Sembra una statua!
Ah ah! Dal ridere sto per crepar!

FIGARO: *(laughing mockingly)*
Look at Don Bartolo!
He seems like a statue!
I can scarcely stop laughing.

BARTOLO:
Ma, signor....

BARTOLO: *(to the Official)*
But sir....

CORO:
Zitto tu!

CHORUS:
You be quiet!

BARTOLO:
Ma un dottor...

BARTOLO:
But a doctor...

CORO:
Oh, non più!

CHORUS:
No more!

BARTOLO:
Ma se lei...

BARTOLO:
But if you...

CORO:
Non parlar

CHORUS:
Stop talking.

BARTOLO:
Ma vorrei...

BARTOLO:
But I should like...

CORO:
Non gridar.

CHORUS:
Stop shouting.

ROSINA, BARTOLO, BASILIO:
Ma se noi...

ROSINA, BARTOLO, BASILIO:
But if we...

CORO:
Zitti voi.

CHORUS:
You be quiet.

ROSINA, BARTOLO, BASILIO:
Ma se poi...

ROSINA, BARTOLO, BASILIO:
But you ought...

CORO:
Pensiam noi. Vada ognun pei fatti suoi, si finisca d'altercar.

CHORUS:
We think that the bickering has ended, and that everyone should be on his way.

BARTOLO:
Ma sentite...

BARTOLO:
But listen...

TUTTI:
Zitto su! Zitto giù!

ALL:
Keep quiet! Shut up!

BARTOLO:
Ma ascoltate...

BARTOLO:
But listen to me.

TUTTI:
Zitto qua! Zitto là!

ALL:
Quiet here! Quiet there!

Vivace

Mi par d'esser con la testa
in un'orrida fucina,
dove cresce e mai non resta
delle incudini sonore
l'importuno strepitar.

My head seems like it's being
pounded by a smith,
the pouding increases from the sound from
the anvil
and the raging noise doesn't stop..

Alternando questo e quello
pesantissimo martello
fa con barbara armonia
muri e volte rimbombar.
E il cervello, poverello,
già stordito, sbalordito,
non ragiona, si confonde,
si riduce ad impazzar.

It alternates back and forth
like a huge hammer
banging savagely and thunderously
against the walls.
The head becomes wretched,
dazed, stunned,
irrational, confounded,
and is reduced to madness.

ACT II

The library of Dr. Bartolo's house.

BARTOLO:
Ma vedi il mio destino! Quel soldato,
per quanto abbia cercato, niun lo conosce
in tutto il reggimento.
Io dubito eh, cospetto!
Che dubitar?
Scommetto che dal conte Almaviva è stato
qui spedito quel signore ad esplorar della
Rosina il core.
Nemmen in casa propria sicuri si può star!
...Ma io

BARTOLO:
Look at what's happened to me! That
soldier, as much as I investigated, is
unknown to the entire regiment.
Besides, I have awful doubts!
What doubt?
I bet that Count Almaviva sent that man
here to determine the state of Rosina's
affections.
Not even my own house is safe!
But I.....

There is a knocking at the door.

Chi batte? Ehi, chi è di là?
Battono, non sentite!
In casa io son; non v'è timore, aprite.

Who's knocking? Who's there?
They knock, and the servants don't hear!
I'm home, don't worry, I'll open the door.

The Count enters, disguised as the Don Alonso, a music-master,

Andante moderato
COUNT

Pa - ce e   gio - ia   sia con   vo - i,

CONTE:
Pace e gioia sia con voi.

COUNT:
May peace and joy be with you.

BARTOLO:
Mille grazie, non s'incomodi.

BARTOLO:
Thank you, don't trouble yourself.

CONTE:
Gioia e pace per mill'anni!

COUNT:
Joy and peace for a thousand years!

BARTOLO:
Obbligato in verità.
(Questo volto non m'è ignoto, non ravviso
non ricordo, ma quel volto?
Non capisco chi sarà?)

BARTOLO:
Really, I'm much obliged.
(I know that face but I don't recognize or
remember it, but whose face is that?
I can't figure out who it is?)

CONTE:
(Ah, se un colpo è andato a vuoto a gabbar
questo balordo, un novel travestimento più
propizio a me sarà.)
Gioia e pace, pace e gioia!

COUNT:
(If this disguise fails to dupe this fool,
another one, more favorable, will be
necessary.)
Joy and peace, peace and joy!

BARTOLO:
Ho capito. (Oh! ciel! che noia!)

BARTOLO:
I understand. (Heavens, what a pest!)

CONTE:
Gioia e pace, ben di core.

COUNT:
Joy and peace, bless you heart.

BARTOLO:
Basta, basta. per pietà,
(Ma che perfido destino!
Ma che barbara giornata!
Tutti quanti a me davanti!
Che crudel fatalità!)

BARTOLO:
Enough, for heaven's sake!
(What treachery pursues me!
What a cruel day!
Everything's against me!
What a cruel destiny!)

CONTE:
(Il vecchion non mi conosce:
oh, mia sorte fortunata!
Ah, mio ben! Fra pochi istanti
parlerem con libertà.)

COUNT:
(The old man doesn't recognize me.
How fortunate!
How wonderful! In a few moments Rosina
and I will be speaking freely.)

BARTOLO:
Insomma, mio signore, chi è lei si può
sapere?

BARTOLO:
Well sir, I would like to know who you are
and what you want?

CONTE:
Don Alonso, professore di musica ed
allievo di Don Basilio.

COUNT:
I am Don Alonso, professor of music and
student of Don Basilio.

BARTOLO:
Ebbene?

BARTOLO:
And so?

CONTE:
Don Basilio sta male, il poverino, ed in sua
vece.

COUNT:
That poor Don Basilio is ill, and has sent
me in his place.

BARTOLO:
Sta mal? Corro a vederlo

BARTOLO: *(ready to leave)*
Ill? I'll go right away to see him.

CONTE:
Piano, piano. Non è mal così grave.

COUNT: *(detaining him)*
Easy, he's not that gravely ill.

BARTOLO:
(Di costui non mi fido.)
Andiam, andiamo.

BARTOLO:
(I don't trust him.)
Come, let's go.

CONTE:
Ma signore.

COUNT:
But sir.

BARTOLO:
Che c'è?

BARTOLO:
Well, what?

CONTE:
Voleva dirvi.

COUNT: *(whispering)*
I wanted to tell you something.

BARTOLO:
Parlate forte.

BARTOLO:
Speak louder.

CONTE:
Ma...

COUNT:
But...

BARTOLO:
Forte, vi dico.

BARTOLO:
I'm telling you to speak louder.

CONTE:
Ebben, come volete, ma chi sia Don Alonso
apprenderete.

COUNT:
Well, as you wish, but then you'll find out
who Don Alonso is.

Vo' dal conte di Almaviva

(pretends to leave)
I have news about Count Almaviva.

BARTOLO:
Piano, piano! Dite, dite, v'ascolto.

BARTOLO: *(holding him back)*
Softly! Tell me, I can hear you.

CONTE:
Il Conte...

COUNT: *(loudly and angrily)*
The Count...

BARTOLO:
Piano, per carità.

BARTOLO:
Softly, for heaven's sake.

CONTE:
Stamane nella stessa locanda era meco
d'alloggio, ed in mie mani per caso capitò
questo biglietto dalla vostra pupilla a lui
diretto.

COUNT: *(calming down)*
I lodge in the same inn as the Count. This
morning, this letter fell into my hands by
accident; it is a letter from your ward to the
Count.

BARTOLO:
Che vedo! È sua scrittura!

BARTOLO: *(taking the letter)*
What do I see! It's her handwriting!

CONTE:
Don Basilio nulla sa di quel foglio: ed io,
per lui venendo a dar lezione alla ragazza,
volea farmene un merito con voi
perchè con quel biglietto si potrebbe

COUNT:
Don Basilio knows nothing of this letter.
I have come in place of him to give the girl
her lesson. I wanted to serve your interests
by giving you this letter..

BARTOLO:
Che cosa?

BARTOLO:
What do you mean?

CONTE:
Vi dirò s'io potessi parlare alla ragazza,
io creder verbigrazia le farei che me lo diè
del conte un'altra amante, prova
significante, che il conte di Rosina si fa
gioco. E perciò...

COUNT:
I am saying, that if I could talk to the girl,
I believe I can persuade her that the Count
already has another lover, and prove
significantly that he is insincere with
Rosina. And perhaps...

BARTOLO:
Piano un poco, una calunnia! Oh bravo!
Degno e vero scolar di Don Basilio!

BARTOLO:
Softly, this is a scandal! Wonderful!
You are a worthy and true disciple of Don
Basilio!

Bartolo embraces him, and then puts the letter in his pocket.

Io saprò come merita ricompensar sì bel
suggerimento.
Vo a chiamar la ragazza;
poichè tanto per me v'interessate,
mi raccomando a voi.

Be assured that I will compensate you well
for your worthy suggestion.
I'm going to call the girl, since you have
my interests in mind,
I am at your service.

CONTE:
Non dubitate.

COUNT:
Have no doubt.

As Bartolo leaves to fetch Rosina, the Count meditates about the progress of his intrigue.

L'affare del biglietto dalla bocca m'è uscito
non volendo.
Ma come far? Senza d'un tal ripiego
mi toccava andar via come un baggiano.

The business of the letter slipped from my
mouth against my will.
But what could I do? Without that pretext,
he would have thrown me out as a pretender.

Il mio disegno a lei ora paleserò; s'ella
acconsente, io son felice appieno.
Eccola. Ah, il cor sento balzarmi in seno.

I'll now reveal my intentions to her; if she
accepts me, I'll be overjoyed.
Here she comes. Oh, how I feel my heart
beating.

BARTOLO:
Venite, signorina. Don Alonso,
che qui vedete, or vi darà lezione.

BARTOLO: *(leading Rosina)*
Come, young lady. Don Alonso, whom you
see here, will give you your lesson.

ROSINA:
Ah!

BARTOLO:
Cos'è stato?

ROSINA:
È un granchio al piede.

CONTE:
Oh nulla: sedete a me vicin, bella fanciulla.
Se non vi spiace, un poco di lezione,
di Don Basilio invece, vi darò.

ROSINA:
Oh, con mio gran piacer la prenderò.

CONTE:
Che volete cantare?

ROSINA:
Io canto, se le aggrada,
il rondò dell'Inutil Precauzione.

BARTOLO:
E sempre, sempre in bocca
l'Inutil Precauzione!

ROSINA:
Io ve l'ho detto: è il titolo dell'opera novella.

BARTOLO:
Or bene, intesi; andiamo.

ROSINA:
Eccolo qua.

ROSINA: (shocked *at seeing the Count)*
Oh!

BARTOLO:
What's the matter?

ROSINA:
It's a cramp in my foot.

COUNT:
It's nothing. Sit next to me, beautiful young
lady. If you don't mind, I'll give you your
lesson instead of Don Basilio.

ROSINA:
Oh, with the greatest pleasure.

COUNT:
What would you like to sing?

ROSINA:
I'll sing, if you don't mind, the Rondo from
the Vain Precaution.

BARTOLO:
She's always, always talking about the Vain
Precaution.

ROSINA:
I have told you, it's the title of a new opera.

BARTOLO:
O.K. then, let's begin.

ROSINA:
Here it is.

The Count seats himself at the clavichord. Bartolo takes a seat to listen.

CONTE:
Da brava, incominciamo.

ROSINA:
Contro un cor che accende amore
di verace, invitto ardore,
s'arma invan poter tiranno
di rigor, di crudeltò.

COUNT:
Wonderful, now let's begin.

ROSINA:
Against a heart in which passionate,
enduring true love has fallen,
the tyrant's vigorous oppression and cruelty
are in vain.

D'ogni assalto vincitore
sempre amor trionferò.

From every assault,
victorious love will triumph.

Ah Lindoro, mio tesoro,
se sapessi, se vedessi!
Questo cane di tutore,
ah, che rabbia che mi fa!
Caro, a te mi raccomando,
tu mi salva, per pietà.

Oh Lindoro, my treasure,
that you may know, that you may see!
This hounding guardian,
has brought me such anguish!
My dearest, I implore you,
to liberate me, for mercy's sake.

CONTE:
Non temer, ti rassicura;
sorte amica a noi sarà.

COUNT: *(aside to Rosina)*
Don't worry, I assure you,
we'll change your fate.

ROSINA:
Dunque spero?

ROSINA:
You mean there's hope?

CONTE:
A me t'affida.

COUNT:
Have faith in me.

ROSINA:
E il mio cor?

ROSINA:
And what about my heart?

CONTE:
Giubilerà.

COUNT:
It will glow.

ROSINA:
Cara immagine ridente,
dolce idea d'un lieto amore,
tu m'accendi in petto il core,
tu mi porti a delirar.

ROSINA:
Precious smiling vision,
gentle idea of blissful love,
you inflame my heart,
you bring me to ecstasy.

CONTE:
Bella voce! Bravissima!

COUNT:
What a beautiful voice! Fantastic!

ROSINA:
Oh! Mille grazie!

ROSINA:
Oh, thank you so much!

BARTOLO:
Certo, bella voce, ma quest'aria, cospetto!
È assai noiosa; la musica a' miei tempi era
altra cosa.
Ah! Quando, per esempio,
cantava Caffariello quell'aria portentosa la,
ra, la sentite. Don Alonso: eccola qua.

BARTOLO:
It sure is a beautiful voice, but this aria is
just awful! It's very annoying. In my time, ,
music was something else.
For example, when Caffariello sung that
wonderful aria, you didn't just hear la, ra,
la. It was like this, Don Alonso, let me
show you.

Quando mi sei vicina,
amabile Rosina.
L'aria dicea Giannina,
ma io dico Rosina.

When you are near me,
my sweet Rosina.
The aria says Giannina,
but I say Rosina.

While Bartolo sings, Figaro enters with a basin under his arms.
He places himself behind Bartolo and mimics him.

Il cor mi brilla in petto,
mi balla il minuetto.

My heart is exploding in my breast,
it is dancing a minuet.

BARTOLO:
Bravo, signor barbiere, ma bravo!

BARTOLO:
Great Mr. Barber, really wonderful!

FIGARO:
Eh, niente affatto: scusi, son debolezze.

FIGARO:
Oh nothing. Please excuse me, I'm sick..

BARTOLO:
Ebben, qui dunque che vieni a fare?

BARTOLO:
Well then, why have you come here?

FIGARO:
Oh bella!
Vengo a farvi la barba: oggi vi tocca.

FIGARO:
Why! I have come to shave you: today is
your day.

BARTOLO:
Oggi non voglio.

BARTOLO:
I don't want a shave today.

FIGARO:
Oggi non vuol? Domani non potrò io.

FIGARO:
Not today? I can't do it tomorrow.

BARTOLO:
Perchè?

BARTOLO:
Why not?

FIGARO:
Perche' ho da fare a tutti gli Ufficiali
del nuovo reggimento barba e testa alla
marchesa Andronica il biondo parrucchin coi
maronè al contino Bombè il ciuffo a
campanile purgante all'avvocato Bernardone
che ieri s'ammalò d'indigestione e poi e poi
che serve.
Dornan non posso.

FIGARO: *(referring to his appointments)*
Because I have appointments to shave all
the officers of the regiment, care for the
wig for the Marquess Andronica, hairdress
the Count Bombè, and give medicine to the
lawyer Bernardone who yesterday came
down with indigestion, and a lot of other
things I have to take care of.
I can't tomorrow.

BARTOLO:
Orsù, meno parole.
Oggi non vo' far barba.

BARTOLO:
Well, no more talking.
Today, I don't want a shave.

FIGARO:
No? Cospetto!
Guardate che avventori!
Vengo stamane: in casa v'è l'inferno
ritorno dopo pranzo.
"Oggi non voglio."
Ma che? M'avete preso
per un qualche barbier da contadini?
Chiamate pur un altro, io me ne vado.

FIGARO:
No? Too bad!
Look at what has happened!
When I came to the house this morning and
it was in an uproar. So I returned after
dinner. "Today I don't want a shave."
What is this? Are you comparing me to a
barber from the countryside?
Get another barber, I'm leaving.

Figaro, feigning indignation, takes his basin and prepares to leave.

BARTOLO:
Che serve? A modo suo; vedi che fantasia!
Va in camera a pigliar la biancheria.
No, vado io stesso.

BARTOLO:
What nonsense? Have it your way!
Go to the room and get towels.
No, I'll go myself.

*Bartolo takes a bunch of keys, first gives them to Figaro,
becomes doubtful, and then takes them back.*

FIGARO:
(Ah, se mi dava in mano il mazzo delle
chiavi, ero a cavallo.)

Dite: non è fra quelle la chiave che apre
quella gelosia?

FIGARO: *(to himself)*
(If I would have that bunch of keys in my
hands, we'd be on our way.)

(aside to Rosina)
Tell me. Isn't the key that opens the
veranda among them?

ROSINA:
Sì, certo; è la piò nuova.

ROSINA:
Yes, it's the newest one.

BARTOLO:
(Ah, son pur buono a lasciar qua quel
diavolo di barbiere!)

BARTOLO: *(reentering)*
(It was not a good idea to leave her with
that rascal barber!)

Bartolo gives Figaro the keys and sends him to fetch the linens.

Animo, va tu stesso.
Passato il corridor, sopra l'armadio
il tutto troverai.
Bada, non toccar nulla

Here Figaro, you go.
You'll find everything in the closet past the
corridor, above the armoire.
Be careful, and don't touch anything.

FIGARO:
Eh? Non son matto.
(Allegri!) Vado e torno.
(Il colpo è fatto.)

FIGARO:
What? I'm no idiot.
(What luck!) I'll be right back.
(Our victory is certain.)

BARTOLO:
È quel briccon, che al Conte ha portato il biglietto di Rosina.

BARTOLO: *(aside to the Count)*
He's the rascal who delivered Rosina's letter to the Count.

CONTE:
Mi sembra un imbroglion di prima sfera.

COUNT:
He seems to be a first-class intriguer.

BARTOLO:
Eh, a me non me la ficca.

BARTOLO:
But he can't delude me.

A thunderous crash is heard.

Ah, disgraziato me!

What in the world was that!

ROSINA:
Ah, che rumore!

ROSINA:
What a crash!

BARTOLO:
Oh, che briccon! Me lo diceva il core.

BARTOLO: *(investigating the crash)*
That scoundrel! I sensed it!

CONTE:
Quel Figaro è un grand'uomo;
or che siam soli, ditemi, o cara: il vostro al
mio destino d'unir siete contenta?
Franchezza!

COUNT: *(to Rosina)*
That Figaro is a terrific man;
but now that we're alone, tell me, my dear,
would you be happy if our destiny is to be
married? Tell me the truth!

ROSINA:
Ah, mio Lindoro, altro io non bramo

ROSINA: *(enthusiastically)*
My, Lindoro, I only want you.

Bartolo and Figaro return.

CONTE:
Ebben?

COUNT:
Well?

BARTOLO:
Tutto mi ha rotto; sei piatti, otto bicchieri,
una terrina.

BARTOLO:
He has broken everything; six plates, eight
glasses, a terrine.

FIGARO:
Vedete che gran cosa! Ad una chiave
se io non mi attaccava per fortuna,
per quel maledettissimo corridor così
oscuro, spezzato mi sarei la testa al muro.

FIGARO: *(showing the key to the Count)*
Look as this! Here's a key that I was
fortunate enough to unattach while in that
awfully lighted corridor, where I almost
broke my head against the wall.

Tiene ogni stanza al buio, e poi e poi

Every room here has its own executioner.

BARTOLO:
Oh, non più.

BARTOLO:
No more of this.

FIGARO:
Dunque andiam.

FIGARO: *(to the Count and Rosina)*
Let's go then.

BARTOLO:
A noi.

BARTOLO: *(to Figaro)*
Let's begin.

Just as Figaro is about to begin shaving Bartolo, Don Basilio arrives.

ROSINA:
Don Basilio!

ROSINA:
Don Basilio!

CONTE:
(Cosa veggo!)

COUNT:
(What do I see!)

FIGARO:
(Quale intoppo!)

FIGARO:
(What a misfortune!)

BARTOLO:
Come qua?

BARTOLO:
How can this be?

BASILIO:
Servitor di tutti quanti.

BASILIO:
Servant to all.

BARTOLO:
(Che vuol dir tal novità?)

BARTOLO:
(What news will we hear now?)

CONTE e FIGARO:
(Qui franchezza ci vorrà.)

COUNT and FIGARO:
(We must be forthright.)

ROSINA:
(Ah, di noi che mai sarà?)

ROSINA:
(What will happen to us?)

BARTOLO:
Don Basilio, come state?

BARTOLO:
Don Basilio, How do you feel?

BASILIO:
Come sto?

BASILIO: *(astonished)*
How do I feel?

FIGARO:
Or che s'aspetta? Questa barba benedetta
la facciamo sì o no?

FIGARO: *(to Bartolo)*
What are you waiting for?
Do we do this beautiful beard? Yes or no?

BARTOLO:
Ora vengo!

BARTOLO:
In a moment!

E il Curiale?

(to Basilio)
And the lawyer?

BASILIO:
Il Curiale?

BASILIO: *(astonished)*
The lawyer?

CONTE:
Io gli ho narrato che già tutto è combinato.
Non è ver?

COUNT: *(interrupting)*
I told him already that everything is taken
care of. Right?

BARTOLO:
Sì, tutto io sò.

BARTOLO:
Yes, I know everything.

BASILIO:
Ma, Don Bartolo, spiegatevi

BASILIO:
But, Don Bartolo, explain yourself.

CONTE:
Ehi, Dottore, una parola.

Don Basilio, son da voi.

Ascoltate un poco qua.
(Fate un po' ch'ei vada via, ch'ei ci scopra
ho gran timore:
della lettera, signore, ei l'affare ancor non
sa.)

COUNT: *(to Bartolo)*
Hey, Doctor, I'd like a word with you.
(to Basilio)
Don Basilio, I'll be with you.
(to Bartolo)
Listen to me for a moment.
(to Figaro) (Make him go away, I have a
great fear he'll discover us.
(to Bartolo) He knows nothing about the
letter.)

BARTOLO:
(Dite bene, mio signore;
or lo mando via di qua.)

BARTOLO:
(Well said, my friend, we'll send him away
from here.)

ROSINA:
(Io mi sento il cor tremar!)

ROSINA:
(I feel my heart trembling!)

FIGARO:
(Non vi state a disperar.)

FIGARO:
(Don't give up hope.)

BASILIO:
(Ah, qui certo v'è un pasticcio;
non l'arrivo a indovinar.)

BASILIO:
(There's certainly a mess here; but I can't
figure it out.)

CONTE:
Colla febbre, Don Basilio,
che v'insegna a passeggiar?

COUNT: *(to Basilio)*
Don Basilio, who told you to go out with a
fever?

BASILIO:
Colla febbre?

BASILIO: *(astonished)*
With a fever?

CONTE:
E che vi pare?
Siete giallo come un morto.

COUNT:
What do you think it is?
You're as yellow as a corpse.

BASILIO:
Come un morto?

BASILIO:
As a corpse?

FIGARO:
Bagattella!
Cospetton! Che tremarella!
Questa è febbre scarlattina!

FIGARO: *(feeling Basilio's pulse)*
Heavens man!
How awful! What shaking!
This is scarlet fever!

CONTE:
Via, prendete medicina, non vi state a rovinar.

COUNT: *(sneaking a purse to Basilio)*
Here, take medicine. Don't stay here and get into bed.

FIGARO:
Presto, presto, andate a letto.

FIGARO:
Quickly, get into bed.

CONTE:
Voi paura inver mi fate.

COUNT:
I'm worried by the way you look.

ROSINA:
Dice bene, andate, andate

ROSINA:
Yes, get into bed.

TUTTI:
Presto, andate a riposar.

ALL:
Quickly, get some rest.

BASILIO:
(Una borsa! Andate a letto!
Ma che tutti sian d'accordo!)

BASILIO: *(astonished)*
(A purse! Go to bed!
And they all seem to agree!)

TUTTI:
Presto a letto.

ALL:
Quick, home to bed.

BASILIO:
Eh, non son sordo.
Non mi faccio più pregar.

BASILIO:
I'm not deaf.
Don't make me pray now.

FIGARO:
Che color!

FIGARO:
What a color!

CONTE:
Che brutta cera!

COUNT:
What an ugly look!

BASILIO:
Brutta cera!

BASILIO:
An ugly look!

CONTE, FIGARO e BARTOLO:
Oh, brutta assai!

COUNT, FIGARO and BARTOLO:
So ugly!

BASILIO:
Dunque vado.

BASILIO:
Therefore, I am going.

TUTTI:
Vada, vada!

ALL:
Go, go!

Moderato
COUNT

Buo - na   se   -   ra, mio   si - gno - re,

Buona sera, mio signore,
presto, andate via di qua.
(Maledetto seccatore!)
Pace, sonno e sanità.

Good evening, my dear sir,
quickly, leave here.
(Damned pest!)
Peace, sweet dreams and health.

BASILIO:
Buona sera ben di core
poi diman si parlerà.
Non gridate, ho inteso già.

BASILIO:
Good evening, good hearted man,
then I'll talk to you tomorrow.
Don't shout, I already understand.

Basilio leaves.

FIGARO:
Orsù, signor Don Bartolo

FIGARO:
Now, Don Bartolo.

BARTOLO:
Son qua.

BARTOLO:
I'm ready.

Bartolo sits in a chair. Figaro ties a towel around his neck
and prepares to shave him.
Figaro stands before Bartolo so he cannot see the two lovers.

Stringi, bravissimo.   Great, nice and tight.

CONTE:
Rosina, deh, ascoltatemi.

COUNT:
Rosina, listen to me.

ROSINA:
Vi ascolto; eccomi qua.

ROSINA:
I'm listening. I'm here.

The Count and Rosina sit at the harpsichord, pretending to study the music.

CONTE:
A mezzanotte in punto a prendervi qui
siamo: or che la chiave abbiamo
non v'è da dubitar.

COUNT: *(cautiously to Rosina)*
At exactly midnight we're coming here to
get you. Now that we have the key there's
no doubt about that.

FIGARO:
Ahi! ahi!

FIGARO: *(distracting Bartolo)*
Ay! Ay!

BARTOLO:
Che cos'è stato?

BARTOLO:
What's happening?

FIGARO:
Un non so che nell'occhio!
Guardate non toccate soffiate per pietà

FIGARO: *(pretending)*
Something flew into my eye!
Look but don't touch.

ROSINA:
A mezzanotte in punto, anima mia,
t'aspetto.
Io già l'istante affretto che a te mi stringerà.

ROSINA:
At exactly midnight, my love, I'll await
you.
I can't wait for you to hold me.

CONTE:
Ora avvertir vi voglio.
Cara, che il vostro foglio, perchè non fosse
inutile il mio travestimento.

COUNT:
Now I do want to caution you my dear.
I showed your letter in order to disguise
myself better.

Overcome by suspicion, Bartolo rises from the chair and approaches the lovers.

BARTOLO:
Il suo travestimento?
Ah, ah! Brava, bravissimo!
Ma bravi in verità!
Briccioni, birbanti!
Ah, voi tutti quanti avete giurato
di farmi crepar!
Su, fuori, furfanti,
vi voglio accoppar.
Di rabbia, di sdegno
mi sento crepar.

BARTOLO:
Your disguise?
Great, terrific!
In truth just great!
Rascals, scoundrels!
All of you swore to bury me!

Get up, get out, scoundrels,
I'd like to beat you to death.
I feel like burying you
because of my anger and scorn.

ROSINA, CONTE e FIGARO:
L'amico delira,
la testa gli gira.
Ma zitto, Dottore,
vi fate burlar.
Tacete, tacete,
non serve gridar.

ROSINA, COUNT and FIGARO:
The man raves,
and his head is spinning.
But quiet, Doctor,
you're making a fool of yourself.
Quiet, quiet,
it's not worth shouting.

Intesi già siamo,
non vo' replicar.)

We understand everything,
you don't have to repeat.

All exit except Bartolo.

BARTOLO:
Ah! Disgraziato me! Ma come!
Ed io no mi accorsi di nulla!
Ah! Don Basilio sa certo qualche cosa.
Ehi! Chi è di là? Chi è di là?

BARTOLO:
What a disgrace! But how could it be that
I wasn't aware of anything!
Don Basilio certainly knows something.
Who's out there? Who's there?

The servants, Ambrosio and Berta, appear.

Senti, Ambrosio:
corri da Don Basilio qui rimpetto,
digli ch'io qua l'aspetto,
che venga immantinente
che ho gran cose da dirgli e ch'io non vado
perchè ho di gran ragioni.
Va' subito.

Listen, Ambrosio:
run over to Don Basilio right now.
Tell him I'm waiting for him and
that he must come immediately,
that I have important matters to tell him,
and that I can't come to him because I
have important reasons. Go immediately.

After Ambrosio exits, Bartolo instructs Berta.

Di guardia tu piantati alla porta, e poi no.
(Non me ne fido.) Io stesso ci starò.

Watch and guard the door
(I don't trust her.) I'll do it myself.

Bartolo exits.

BERTA:
Che vecchio sospettoso! Vada pure
e ci stia finchè crepa!
Sempre gridi e tumulti in questa casa;
si litiga, si piange, si minaccia
Non v'è un'ora di pace
con questo vecchio avaro, brontolone!

BERTA:
That old suspicious fool! First he
commands me and than not!
There's always shouting and tumult in this
house; quarrels, crying, and threatening.
Not an hour of peace with this old stingy
grumbler!

Oh, che casa! Oh, che casa in confusione!
Il vecchiotto cerca moglie,
vuol marito la ragazza;
quello freme, questa è pazza.
Tutti e due son da legar.
Ma che cosa è questo amore
che fa tutti delirar?
Egli è un male universale,
una smania, un pizzicore
un solletico, un tormento
Poverina, anch'io lo sento,
nè so come finirà.

What a house! What a house of confusion!
The old man seeks a wife,
wants to marry a young girl,
and all that fretting, this is crazy.
Everyone is crazy.
But what is this love that makes all of them
delirious?
It is a universal evil,
a frenzy, an itch,
anxiety, torment.
The poor girl, I feel for her,
but I don't know how it will end.

Oh! Vecchiaia maledetta
Sei da tutti disprezzata
E vecchietta disperata
mi convien così crepar.

Damned ageing.
I'm such a spiteful
and despairing old woman,
perhaps it would be better to die.

Berta exits.

A room with barred windows. Bartolo and Basilio converse.

BARTOLO:
Dunque voi Don Alonso non conoscete affatto?

BARTOLO:
So about this Don Alonso, you don't know him at all?

BASILIO:
Affatto.

BASILIO:
Nothing.

BARTOLO:
Ah, certo il Conte lo mandò.
Qualche gran tradimento qui si prepara.

BARTOLO:
Surely the Count sent him to organize some treachery.

BASILIO:
Io poi dico che quell'amico era il Conte in persona.

BASILIO:
But I tell you that man was the Count himself.

BARTOLO:
Il Conte?

BARTOLO:
The Count himself?

BASILIO:
Il Conte.
(La borsa parla chiaro.)

BASILIO:
The Count.
(The purse revealed it to me clearly.)

BARTOLO:
Sia chi si vuole amico, dal notaro
vo' in questo punto andare; in questa sera
stipular di mie nozze io vo' il contratto.

BARTOLO:
If that's true, I want you to go right away
and get the notary, and stipulate that I want
the marriage contract this evening.

BASILIO:
Il notar? Siete matto?
Piove a torrenti, e poi questa sera il notaro
è impegnato con Figaro; il barbiere
marita sua nipote.

BASILIO:
The notary? Are you crazy?
It's raining and storming, and besides, this
evening the notary is committed to Figaro,
the barber, for his niece's marriage.

BARTOLO:
Una nipote? Che nipote!
Il barbiere non ha nipoti.
Ah, qui v'è qualche imbroglio.

BARTOLO:
A niece? What niece!
The barber has no nieces.
Ah, there's some intrigue going on here.

Questa notte i bricconi me la voglion far; presto, il notaro qua venga sull'istante.

This evening the rascals will try to betray me. So go quickly, and bring the notary right away.

Bartolo gives Basilio a key to the house.

Ecco la chiave del portone: andate, presto, per carità.

Here's the door key: go quickly, for heaven's sake.

BASILIO:
Non temete; in due salti io torno qua.

BASILIO:
Don't worry, I'll return right away.

Basilio exits.

BARTOLO:
Per forza o per amore
Rosina avrà da cedere. Cospetto!
Mi viene un'altra idea.

BARTOLO:
Either by force, or for love
Rosina will have to concede. Besides!
I have another idea.

Bartolo takes the letter from his pocket.

Questo biglietto che scrisse la ragazza ad Almaviva potria servir che colpo da maestro! Don Alonso, il briccone, senza volerlo mi diè l'armi in mano.
Ehi, Rosina, Rosina, avanti, avanti.

This letter that the girl wrote to Almaviva will serve to provide the master stroke! Don Alonso, that rascal, without wanting to, put ammunition in my hand.
Hey, Rosina, come here.

Rosina enters without talking.

Del vostro amante io vi vo' dar novella.
Povera sciagurata!
In verità collocaste assai bene il vostro affetto!
Del vostro amor sappiate ch'ei si fa gioco in sen d'un'altra amante.
Ecco la prova.

I have news about your lover.
Unfortunate girl!
You should know the truth about where you have placed your affections!
You should know that your love is playing a game with you and has another lover.
Here is the proof.

Bartolo gives Rosina the letter.

ROSINA:
(Oh cielo! Il mio biglietto!)

ROSINA:
(Heavens, my letter!)

BARTOLO:
Don Alonso e il barbiere congiuran contro voi; non vi fidate.
Nelle braccia del Conte d'Almaviva vi vogliono condurre.

BARTOLO:
Don Alonso and the barber conspired against you, don't trust them.
They wanted to lead you into the arms of the Count Almaviva.

ROSINA:
(In braccio a un altro!)

ROSINA:
(In the arms of another!)

Che mai sento ah, Lindoro! Ah, traditore!
Ah si! vendetta!
E vegga quell'empio chi è Rosina.)

Dite signore, di sposarmi voi bramavate

BARTOLO:
E il voglio.

ROSINA:
Ebben, si faccia!
Io son contenta! Ma all'istante.
Udite: a mezzanotte qui sarà l'indegno
con Figaro il barbier, con lui fuggire
per sposarlo io voleva.

BARTOLO:
Ah, scellerati!
Corro a sbarrar la porta.

ROSINA:
Ah, mio signore!
Entran per la finestra. Hanno la chiave.

BARTOLO:
Non mi muovo di qui.
Ma e se fossero armati? Figlia mia,
poichè tu sei sì bene illuminata
facciam così.
Chiuditi a chiave in camera, io vo a
chiamar la forza;
dirò che son due ladri, e come tali,
corpo di Bacco! L'avrem da vedere!
Figlia, chiuditi presto; io vado via.

What do I hear. Oh, Lindoro, a traitor!
Yes, vengeance!
Rosina will punish that impious one.)

Tell me sir, do you still desire to marry me.

BARTOLO:
Yes I do.

ROSINA:
Well, you can!
I am content! But right way!
Listen. At midnight that disgraceful man
and Figaro the barber will come here. I
wanted to flee with him and marry him.

BARTOLO:
Scoundrels!
I'll bar the entrance door.

ROSINA:
Oh no, sir! They'll enter by the balcony
door. They have the key.

BARTOLO:
I won't move from here.
But should I be armed? My dear child,
because there is too much light, here's
what we can do.
Lock yourself in your room, and I'll go to
call the police;
I'll say there are two robbers, and as such,
they'll have to come to investigate!
Child, lock it quickly, I'm on my way.

Bartolo exits.

ROSINA:
Quanto, quanto è crudel la sorte mia!

ROSINA:
My destiny is so, oh so cruel!

Rosina exits.

A storm rages. From the window flashes of lightning are seen, and thunder is heard.
When the storm subsides, the shutters are opened from the outside, and Figaro, followed
by the Count, enters by the balcony door.
They are both wrapped in cloaks, and Figaro carries a lantern.

FIGARO:
Alfin, eccoci qua.

CONTE:
Figaro, dammi man. Poter del mondo!
Che tempo indiavolato!

FIGARO:
Tempo da innamorati.

CONTE:
Ehi, fammi lume.

Dove sarà Rosina?

FIGARO:
Ora vedremo Eccola appunto.

CONTE:
Ah, mio tesoro!

ROSINA:
Indietro,
anima scellerata; io qui di mia
stolta credulità venni soltanto
a riparar lo scorno, a dimostrarti
qual sono, e quale amante
perdesti, anima indegna e sconoscente.

CONTE:
Io son di sasso.

FIGARO:
Io non capisco niente.

CONTE:
Ma per pietà.

ROSINA:
Taci. Fingesti amore per vendermi alle
voglie di quel tuo vil Conte Almaviva

CONTE:
Al Conte?
Ah, sei delusa! Oh me felice adunque
tu di verace amore ami Lindor?
Rispondi!

FIGARO:
Finally, we are here.

COUNT:
Figaro, give me a hand. Power of the
world! What a tempestuous night!

FIGARO:
Truly a time lovers.

COUNT:
Hey, give me light.

Where is Rosina?

FIGARO: *(spying about)*
Now we'll see. There she is.

COUNT: *(finding Rosina)*
Oh, My treasure!

ROSINA: *(repelling him)*
Go, get away.
villainous soul; I, with my foolish honesty,
waited here only to mend the scorn, and
show you what I am, and the loved one you
have lost, you deceiver and unappreciative
man.

COUNT: *(surprised)*
I'm petrified.

FIGARO:
I don't understand a thing.

COUNT:
For heaven's sake.

ROSINA:
Quiet. You pretended love so you could sell
me to the whims of the vile Count Almaviva.

COUNT: *(with joy)*
To the Count?
You're deluded! How happy I am.
Therefore, your true love is Lindoro?
Answer me!

ROSINA:
Ah, sì! T'amai pur troppo!

ROSINA:
Yes! I love him so much!

CONTE:
Ah, non è tempo di più celarsi, anima mia;
ravvisa...

COUNT:
There's no more time to disguise it, my
love, look...

The Count throws off his cloak, kneels before Rosina, and reveals his true identity.

Colui che sì gran tempo seguò tue tracce, che
per te sospira, che sua ti vuole; mira, o mio
tesoro, Almaviva son io, non son Lindoro.

For a long time I followed your steps,
I sighed for you, I yearned for you. Look,
my treasure, I am Almaviva, not Lindoro.

ROSINA:
(Ah! qual colpo inaspettato!
Egli stesso? O Ciel, che sento!
Di sorpresa e di contento
son vicina a delirar.)

ROSINA: *(stupefied and joyful)*
(What an unexpected surprise!
Him? Oh Heavens what do I feel!
Surprise and contentment are bringing me
to ecstasy.)

FIGARO:
(Son rimasti senza fiato: ora muoion di
contento.
Guarda, guarda il mio talento che bel colpo
seppe far!)

FIGARO:
I remain breathless: now the displeasure
ends.
Look, how my talents have made such a
beautiful event happen!)

CONTE:
(Qual trionfo inaspettato!
Me felice! Oh bel momento!
Ah! D'amore e di contento
son vicina a delirar.)

COUNT:
(What an unexpected triumph!
I am so happy! Oh what a beautiful
moment! Love and contentment are
bringing me to ecstasy.)

ROSINA:
Mio signor! Ma voi ma io

ROSINA:
Sir! But you...but I..

CONTE:
Ah, non più, non più, ben mio.
Il bel nome di mia sposa,
idol mio, t'attende già.

COUNT:
Oh, no more, you are mine.
The name of my wife and loved one, my
treasure, awaits you.

ROSINA:
Il bel nome di tua sposa
oh, qual gioia al cor mi dà!

ROSINA:
To be called your wife,
brings such joy to my heart!

CONTE:
Sei contenta!

COUNT:
Be happy!

ROSINA:
Ah! Mio signore!

ROSINA:
Oh, my lord!

ROSINA e CONTE:
Dolce nodo avventurato
che fai paghi i miei desiri!
Alla fin de' miei martiri
tu sentisti, amor, pietà.

ROSINA and COUNT:
Oh happy bonds of love
that will satisfy my wishes and desires!
If we wait too long, all our efforts
will be wasted.

FIGARO:
Presto andiamo, vi sbrigate;
via, lasciate quei sospiri.
Se si tarda, i miei raggiri
fanno fiasco in verità.

FIGARO:
Quickly, let's go, hurry;
come on, leave those sighs.
If we're late, my scheme
will truthfully become a fiasco.

Figaro looks outside.

Ah! Cospetto! Che ho veduto?
Alla porta una lanterna
due persone! Che si fa?

My goodness! What do I see?
There are two people at the door with a
lantern! What now?

CONTE:
Hai veduto due persone?

COUNT:
You've seen two people?

FIGARO:
Sì, signore.

FIGARO:
Yes, sir.

ROSINA, CONTE e FIGARO:
Che si fa?

ROSINA, COUNT and FIGARO:
What do we do now?

Allegro
COUNT

Zit-ti   zit - ti,   pia - no   pia - no,   non facciamo confu - sio - ne;

Zitti, zitti, piano, piano,
non facciamo confusione;
per la scala del balcone
presto andiamo via di qua.

Quietly, softly,
with no commotion;
we'll quickly go down
the balcony ladder from here.

FIGARO:
Ah, disgraziati noi! Come si fa?

FIGARO: *(with anxiety)*
We are disgraced! How did it happen?

CONTE:
Che avvenne mai?

COUNT:
What happened?

FIGARO:
La scala

FIGARO:
The ladder.

CONTE:
Ebben?

COUNT:
Well?

FIGARO:
La scala non v'è più.

FIGARO:
The ladder is gone.

CONTE:
Che dici?

COUNT:
What did you say?

FIGARO:
Chi mai l'avrà levata?

FIGARO:
Who might have taken it away?

CONTE:
Quale inciampo crudel!

COUNT:
What a cruel joke!

ROSINA:
Me sventurata!

ROSINA:
My misfortune!

FIGARO:
Zi zitti sento gente. Ora ci siamo.
Signor mio, che si fa?

FIGARO:
Quiet, people. Someone is coming.
My lord, what now?

CONTE:
Mia Rosina, coraggio.

COUNT:
Courage, my dear Rosina.

Rosina wraps herself in the Count's cloak.

FIGARO:
Eccoli qua.

FIGARO:
Here they are.

Figaro, the Count, and Rosina hide as Don Basilio and a notary enter.

BASILIO:
Don Bartolo! Don Bartolo!

BASILIO:.
Don Bartolo! Don Bartolo!

FIGARO:
Don Basilio.

FIGARO:
Don Basilio.

CONTE:
E quell'altro?

COUNT:
And who else?

FIGARO:
Ve', ve', il nostro notaro. Allegramente.
Lasciate fare a me.

FIGARO:
Look, our notary. Perfect.
Leave everything to me.

Signor Notaro: dovevate in mia casa
stipular questa sera il contratto di nozze
fra il conte d'Almaviva e mia nipote.
Gli sposi, eccoli qua.
Avete indosso la scrittura?

Mister Notary. Remember that this evening
in my house you made the marriage
contract between Almaviva and my niece.
Well, the bride and groom are here. Do you
have the paper?

The notary takes out a paper.

Benissimo.

Perfect.

BASILIO:
Ma piano.
Don Bartolo dov'è?

BASILIO:
But slow down.
Where is Don Bartolo?

The Count takes Basilio aside and indicates that he should be silent.
To convince him, the Count gives him a ring.

CONTE:
Ehi, Don Basilio, quest'anello è per voi

COUNT:
Here, Don Basilio, this ring is for you.

BASILIO:
Ma io...

BASILIO:
But I...

CONTE:
Per voi vi son ancor due palle nel cervello
se v'opponete.

COUNT: *(taking out a pistol)*
There'll be two shots in your head if you
oppose.

BASILIO:
Oibò, prendo l'anello.
Chi firma?

BASILIO: *(taking the ring)*
Okay, I'll take the ring.
Who signs?

CONTE e ROSINA:
Eccoci qua.

COUNT and ROSINA:
Here we are.

(The contract is signed)

CONTE:
Son testimoni Figaro e Don Basilio.
Essa è mia sposa.

COUNT:
Figaro and Don Basilio are witness that this
woman is now my wife.

FIGARO e BASILIO:
Evviva!

FIGARO and BASILIO:
Hail!

CONTE:
Oh, mio contento!

COUNT:
I am so delighted!

ROSINA:
Oh, sospirata mia felicità!

ROSINA:
A deep sigh of happiness!

FIGARO:
Evviva!

FIGARO:
Hail!

While the Count kisses Rosina's hand, Figaro brusquely embraces Basilio.
Suddenly Dr. Bartolo enters with an Officer and a patrol of soldiers.

BARTOLO:
Fermi tutti. Eccoli qua.

BARTOLO:
All of you hold it. Here they are.

UFFIZIALE:
Colle buone, signor.

OFFICER:
Good sir.

BARTOLO:
Signor, son ladri.
Arrestate, arrestate.

BARTOLO:
They are robbers.
Arrest them.

UFFIZIALE:
Mio signore, il suo nome?

OFFICIAL: *(to the Count)*
Sir, your name?

CONTE:
Il mio nome è quel d'un uom d'onor.
Lo sposo io sono di questa

COUNT:
My name is one of honor.
I am the husband of this lady.

BARTOLO:
Eh, andate al diavolo! Rosina
esser deve mia sposa: non è vero?

BARTOLO:
Go to the devil! Rosina is going to be my
wife, isn't that right?

ROSINA:
Io sua sposa? Oh, nemmeno per pensiero.

ROSINA:
Your wife? Don't give it a thought.

BARTOLO:
Come? Come, fraschetta?
Arrestate, vi dico è un ladro.

BARTOLO: *(pointing to the Count)*
What? What frivolity?
Arrest him, I'm telling you he's a robber.

FIGARO:
Or or l'accoppo.

FIGARO:
Or beat him to death.

BARTOLO:
È un furfante, è un briccon.

BARTOLO:
He's a rascal, a scoundrel.

UFFIZIALE:
Signore

OFFICIAL: *(to the Count)*
Sir.

CONTE:
Indietro!

COUNT:
Get back!

UFFIZIALE:
Il nome?

OFFICIAL:
Your name?

CONTE:
Indietro, dico, indietro

COUNT:
Back, I tell you, back.

UFFIZIALE:
Ehi, mio signor! Basso quel tono.
Chi è lei?

OFFICIAL:
Sir! Lower you voice.
Who are you?

CONTE:
Il Conte d'Almaviva io sono.

COUNT:
I am Count Almaviva.

BARTOLO:
Il Conte! Ah, che mai sento!
Ma cospetto!

BARTOLO:
The Count! What do I hear!
Damned it!

CONTE:
T'accheta, invan t'adopri,
resisti invan.
De' tuoi rigori insani giunse l'ultimo
istante. In faccia al mondo io dichiaro
altamente costei mia sposa.

COUNT:
Be quiet, in vain you exerted yourself, in
vain you resisted.
From your rigorous insanities the ultimate
moment has arrived. Before the world I
declare that Rosina is my wife.

Il nostro nodo, o cara, opra è d'amore.
Amore, che ti fe' mia consorte a te mi
stringerà fino alla morte.
Respira omai: del fido sposo in braccio,
vieni, vieni a goder sorte più lieta.

(to Rosina).
Our bond, dearest, is the work of love.
My love and faith will accompany
you until death.
In the arms of your faithful husband
be assured of a happy future.

BARTOLO:
Ma io...

BARTOLO:
But I...

CONTE:
Taci.

COUNT:
Be quiet.

BASILIO:
Ma voi

BASILIO:
But you.

CONTE:
Olà, t'accheta.
Cessa di più resistere,
non cimentar mio sdegno.
Spezzato è il gioco indegno
di tanta crudeltà.

COUNT:
Be quiet..
Stop resisting,
and don't provoke my rage.
Stop your disgraceful game
of such cruelty.

Della beltà dolente,	From sorrowful beauty,
d'un innocente amore	for innocent love
l'avaro tuo furore	you avaricious furor
più non trionferà.	will no longer triumph.

Andante
COUNT

E   tu,   in - feli - ce   vit - tima d'un reo po - ter   ti - ran - no,

	(to Rosina)
E tu, infelice vittima	And you, unfortunate victim
d'un reo poter tiranno,	of a wicked, tyrannical force,
sottratta al giogo barbaro,	escape from the cruel yoke,
cangia in piacer l'affanno	discover the pleasure and
e in sen d'un fido sposo	rejoice in the freedom
gioisci in libertà. Cari amici	brought to you by a faithful husband.

CORO:	**CHORUS:**
Non temete.	Don't be afraid..

CONTE:	**COUNT:**
Questo nodo.	This marriage.

CORO:	**CHORUS:**
Non si scioglie,	Keep the bonds,
sempre a lei vi stringerà.	always hold it dear.

Moderato
COUNT

Ah il più lie-to, il più fe - li - ce è il   mio cor de' cori a - man - te

CONTE:	**COUNT:**
Ah, il più lieto, il più felice	The most blessed and the happiest
è il mio cor de' cori amanti;	are the hearts of profound lovers;
non fuggite, o lieti istanti	don't escape, blessed moment
della mia felicità.	of my happiness.

CORO:	**CHORUS:**
Annodar due cori amanti	Nothing equals tieing two loving hearts
è piacer che egual non ha.	together.

BARTOLO:
Insomma, io ho tutti i torti

FIGARO:
Eh, purtroppo è così!

BARTOLO:
Ma tu, briccone, tu pur tradirmi e far da testimonio!

BASILIO:
Ah, Don Bartolo mio, quel signor Conte certe ragioni ha in tasca, certi argomenti a cui non si risponde.

BARTOLO:
Ed io, bestia solenne, per meglio assicurare il matrimonio, io portai via la scala del balcone.

FIGARO:
Ecco che fa un'Inutil Precauzione.

BARTOLO:
Ma e la dote? Io non posso...

CONTE:
Eh, via; di dote io bisogno non ho: va, te la dono.

FIGARO:
Ah, ah! Ridete adesso?
Bravissimo, Don Bartolo,
ho veduto alla fin rasserenarsi
quel vostro ceffo amaro e furibondo.
Eh, i briconi han fortuna in questo mondo.

ROSINA:
Dunque, signor Don Bartolo?

BARTOLO:
Sì, sì, ho capito tutto.

CONTE:
Ebben, dottore?

BARTOLO:
In short, everything is my fault.

FIGARO:
Unfortunately that's right!

BARTOLO: *(to Basilio)*
But you, scoundrel, you also betrayed me and were a witness!

BASILIO:
My dear Don Bartolo, that Count had certain reasons in his pocket, and certain arguments with which I could not argue.

BARTOLO:
And I, raging alone, secured the matrimony by removing the ladder from the balcony.

FIGARO:
So it is a Vain Precaution.

BARTOLO:
But the dowry? I cannot...

COUNT:
I have no need for the dowry. I give it to you.

FIGARO:
Ah, now you're smiling?
Terrific, Don Bartolo,
I have finally seen your bitter and angry face cheer up.
Even scoundrels have luck in this world.

ROSINA:
So, Don Bartolo?

BARTOLO:
Yes, I understand everything.

COUNT:
Well, doctor?

BARTOLO:
Sì, sì, che serve? Quel ch'è fatto è fatto.
Andate pur, che il ciel vi benedica.

BARTOLO:
Yes, what does it matter? What has
happened, has happened. May heaven bless
you.

FIGARO:
Bravo, bravo, un abbraccio; venite qua,
dottore.

FIGARO:
Great, let me embrace you.
Come here Doctor.

ROSINA:
Ah, noi felici!

ROSINA:
Oh, we're so happy!

CONTE:
Oh, fortunato amore!

COUNT:
Oh, what a blessed love!

FIGARO:
Di sì felice innesto
serbiam memoria eterna;
io smorzo la lanterna;
qui più non ho che far.

FIGARO:
Let's always remember
this happy moment,
I'll turn off the lantern now,
it is not needed her anymore.

ROSINA:
Costò sospiri e pianti
un sì felice istante:
alfin quest'alma amante
comincia a respirar.

ROSINA:
We've sighed and shed many tears
for the happiness of this moment:
but finally the dreams of lovers
are fulfilled.

CORO:
Amore e fede eterna
si vegga in voi regnar.

CHORUS:
Love and eternal faith
may they reign forever.

FINE

END